ZEN

Key to Your Undiscovered Happiness

ZEN

Key to Your Undiscovered Happiness

C.N. HU

Victory Press

Monterey, CA

Printed in the United States of America.

Library of Congress Cataloging-in-Publication Data
Hu, C. N.
Zen: Key to Your Undiscovered Happiness
Bibliography
Includes index
1. Zen Buddhism--Doctrines.   I. Title
BQ9268.3.H8 1988
294.3'927--dc19   88-20547

ISBN 0-9620765-0-3

Note:

The author conceived the idea for this book during the 1950's. It was written in 1968 and left undisturbed at the bottom of a bookshelf for 20 years.

Due to the recent popularity of the subject, the author has submitted the unchanged manuscript for publication.

During the past 20 years, many things have changed and many advances have been made in science, but the basic concepts of the book still hold.

Editor

Contents

Introduction

What is Zen? And why must we study it in this atomic age? These are probably the first two reactions in the mind of any person who happens to glance over the cover of this book.

Naturally, these are two important questions. Every reader deserves a brief and satisfactory explanation at the beginning. Otherwise, to read this book may mean nothing but a sheer waste of time.

For this reason, the author of this book wishes to use the next few paragraphs to state the basic problems all of us face, and also attempt to offer Zen as their solution. If the observation does not make any sense to the reader, he can discard this book right away. If, on the other hand, it does make some sense to him, he is urged to read as much as he feels like.

The basic problems we face are that we can never get what we want in life. And worse still, our goals constantly change. Once we have reached one goal, we might have something else in mind. In other words, we merely exist. We do not live. We are always in the expectation of living. Because of this pattern of yearning, we are constantly confronted with frustrations. Life turns out to be just a problem solving process. It is quite obvious and everyone can see for himself that there are more failures than successes in life. And furthermore, what we normally consider to be a success in life is,

1

in effect, transitory. There is no permanency whatsoever.

Whether you are a president of a corporation or president of a nation, the presidency can never last forever. No matter who you are, no matter what you are, and no matter how successful you are considered to be, frustration will creep in eventually. And remember, there are only a few people who are tops in each endeavor. These few are just a fraction of the human race. The majority, no matter how hard they have tried, still remain in oblivion.

Now, let us go one step further and analyze the activities in which we are normally engaged. We can break our activities into a few criteria according to our primary drives. They are money, power, position, fame, honor, sentiment, propagation, and self-preservation. Some of these drives are socially encouraged, some are socially accepted, and others are anti-social.

In the pursuit of these goals, it is very easy for us to lose our perspectives. If we work hard enough, we may materialize a few of these objectives. But the problem is that whatever you like to seek, other people like too. Since the competition is so keen and the tension is so great, instead of success we may end up in a mental hospital or lose our life in the process. Is such a tragic ending in our life necessary?

In order to avoid frustration and stop worrying on one hand, and to attain peace and enjoy happiness on the other, we must re-evaluate our mode of living, and we must re-examine our traditional value judgement. Above all, we must re-orient our philosophy of life.

Zen can soothe your tension. Zen can make you regain your perspectives in life. Zen understands and appreciates the intimacy of psychosomatic relations. While stressing mental hygiene, it can offer you physical well-being.

Zen serves like a boat which can help you cross life's torrents safely. It is like a doctor, whom you do not need while healthy; but when you are ill, he is indispensable. When you are frustrated with life's problems, Zen is indispensable.

Keeping psychosis, neurosis and all other mental disorders from you and keeping you serene, contented and free from worrying are just a few practical applications of Zen to our daily living.

From the academic view, it is also very interesting to find out how modern science can interpret and supplement, rather than contradict, religion. This quite unusual point is discussed and substantiated elsewhere in this book.

From the cultural view, it is also interesting to find out how western science can unearth the hidden wisdom of the East. Through Zen, East and West can meet at last.

PART I

THE DHARMA AND ITS INTERPRETATION

CHAPTER 1

WHAT IS ZEN?

Zen is one of ten Buddhistic denominations in China. The word Zen is the Japanese version for the character (禪), romanized as Chan, which was again derived from the Sanskrit word *Dhyana*, meaning meditation. Since the word *Zen* is quite accepted in the English language, it is used in this book in lieu of *Chan*.

Zen, though originated as a religious sect, does not worship God. Nor does it observe any ritual or require any church affiliation. Zen does not quarrel with any religion. In fact, it gets along very well with all religions in the world.

The scriptures Zen believers treasure most are the *Diamond Sutra* and the *Sutra of the Sixth Patriarch*, Hui Neng. The Sanskrit title of the *Diamond Sutra* is *Vajracchedika Sutra*. It is number nine of the *Great Prajna Paramita Sutra*. Hui Neng was Chinese and was the sixth and also last patriarch of the Zen denomination in China.

These two Zen scriptures stress the concept of void or naught which is quite contrary to our ordinary way of thinking. Since this concept is the essence of Zen, it is critically examined in the chapters on reality and language. The reader will see for himself the modern interpretation of this concept.

Buddhism originated in India and is a major religion in the world. People in China, Korea, and

7

Japan on one hand, and in Ceylon, Burma, Siam, etc. on the other, are predominantly Buddhists. But strangely enough, Buddism is not popular in its own native land, India, for reasons to be explained later.

There are two types of Buddhism. One is called Mahayana, or the great vehicle, and the other is called Hinayana, or the small vehicle. Mahayana school spread from China through Korea to Japan. Hinayana school is popular in South East Asia. The major difference between these two schools is that Hinayana Buddism aims at self-salvation whereas Mahayana Buddhism is interested in saving the suffering humanity. A detailed account of Mahayana philosophy will be found in the chapter on compassion.

Most Chinese scholars in China are interested in the teachings of Buddhism in general and Zen Buddhism in particular. These teachings are known as *Fou Hsueh*, (佛學) which can be translated as "Buddhiology". "Buddhiology" is not a religion. It is an objective study of a discipline. Those who study it are not necessarily identified as Buddhists.

The cultural history of China has recorded that Lao Tzu's concept of nature and Confucius' concept of God did contribute considerably to the development of Zen. During the Sung Dynasty, about 1,000 years ago, a new school of philosophy was founded. This school encompassed both Taoist and Buddhist teachings within the framework of the Confucian school of thought. It blended three different schools of philosophy into a synthetic

8

whole. This school is known as the Neo-Confucian school in the history of Chinese philosophy.

In addition to its impact on Chinese thought, Buddhism has also influenced Chinese art, poetry, and architecture. In fact, Buddhism is now quite interwoven into the general pattern of the cultural fabric of the East. Students of oriental languages and area studies should, therefore, study it in its cultural context. Students of psychology will also find it an effective system of psycho-therapy. Students of comparative religion and philosophy will, of course, find the Buddhistic view on reality very unusual.

This book is primarily interested in the philosophical or metaphysical aspect of Buddhism. It is a book on metaphysics. Modern physics deals with the physical world surrounding us. This book on metaphysics attempts to interpret the philosophy of Zen and also hopes to point out the way to happiness at all times. Because of its universal appeal, this writer believes that the reader will find this approach to the study Zen both convincing and interesting.

Chapter 2

The Historical Buddha and His Teachings

In this chapter, the historical Buddha is introduced not so much as the founder of a religion, but as a thinker and psychologist. We are now going to study, analyze, and evaluate his philosophical system and his contribution to man's knowledge.

This author tries not to repeat what other commentators have said in the past that Buddha is great because he is the founder of a major religion, or to urge the reader to believe in his sayings simply because the impact of his system on man's thinking is great.

This author, on the other hand, will employ modern physics and general semantics to prove the validity of his system or the lack of it. The comments will be based strictly on empirical science. In other words, the treatment of Buddha's time honored system in this book will be quite fresh, critical and original.

Before his philosophical system is presented, Buddha's life is summarized herewithin. This author believes that if the reader is familiar with Buddha's background, it will be much easier to follow and appreciate the comments in the following chapters.

The founder of Buddhism was Siddhattha Gotama, born 560 B.C. as a prince of Sakya Kingdom in India. He was about the contemporary

10

of Confucius (551-478 B.C.) in China and about 91 years older than Socrates (469-399B.C.) in ancient Greece.

Since Siddhattha was a prince and his father, the King of Sakya was anxious to see that his son was happy, the youngster was always kept in the beautiful palace. All things unpleasant, sorrowful, or miserable, and even the knowledge of them were kept away from him.

As he grew older, he was not satisfied with the sheltered life he had in the palace. Like other youngsters, he desired to have adventures. After he was married and had a son himself, one day, he managed to get out of the palace. He was eager to see the outside world. When he rode in a carriage and left the palace, his mind was full of curiosity and enthusiasm.

Before long, he saw an old man with bent frame and wrinkled face on the roadside who could not walk very well. As the young prince rode on, again he saw a sick man lying on the road side, gasping for breath and groaning with pain. Before he had time to find out all about the pitiful sight of this sick man, he encountered a corpse, being carried by four men.

The young man was upset by what he saw. He could not help but ask the horseman what happened to these people. With a heavy heart, the horseman replied that every human being has to undergo these stages in life.

After he heard this, the young prince was full of awe and terror. When he returned to the palace, his mind was heavy. He wanted to find out whether or not there was a way to avoid the cycle of birth, decay, disease, and death.

That very night, he could not sleep. The horrible sights he encountered in the daytime bothered him deeply. Finally, he could not stand it. He left his wife and baby, and went out to wander in the wilderness, hoping that he could find a way to salvation.

After many years of search and research, he was said to be enlightened at last. He devoted his later life lecturing to his disciples on the "Middle Path" as a way to salvation. His physical life ended at the age of 80. These are the major events in the life of historical Buddha.

The following is his teaching known as Dharma or the truth. After his enlightenment in the Deer Park at Benares, Buddha made a major speech which was considered one of the most important pronouncements that man had ever made. In this speech or sermon, he made a profound analysis of suffering and its remedy. This analysis is the core of Buddhism, and it has influenced the thinking of mankind for the past 2,500 years.

According to his research, there are four noble truths concerning suffering. Anyone who can recognize the existence of suffering, its cause, its remedy, and its cessation has fathomed the four noble truths.

1. The noble truth concerning the existence of suffering is this: Birth is attended with pain; decay is painful; disease is painful; death is painful. Union with the unpleasant is painful; painful is

separation from the pleasant; any craving that is not satisfied is also painful. In brief,conditions of the body which spring from attachment are painful.

2. The noble truth concerning the origin of suffering is this: It is craving which seeks satisfaction. We crave for gratification of our passions. We crave for a future life. And we crave for happiness in this life.

3. The noble truth concerning the remedy of suffering is this: If we can destroy our desires, if we can be free from passions, then there is no more suffering.

4. The noble truth concerning the way which leads to the destruction of sorrow or suffering is called "The noble eightfold path"; namely, right views, right speech, right aspiration, right behavior, right livelihood, right effort, right thoughts, and right contemplation.

Among these eight items, Buddha believed that the most important and yet most difficult to possess is right views. He considered that we do not hold right views concerning the phenomenal world of ours. What we see as reality is actually a delusion.

"When you are viewing the whole appearance of a country, seeing its mountains, rivers, people, etc., there seem to be discriminated particulars of fact, but in truth they are all made up by the original beginningless sickness of perceiving eyes", he stated in the *Surangama Sutra*.

Buddha does not believe that there is an entity called atman, true self, or soul. He believes that soul is just a functional unity of five components of our body. This view on atman or soul together with his theory on the transmigration of soul is explained in the chapter on language.

In any Buddhistic literature, the name of God has never been mentioned. This conspicuous absence of God is very interesting. Buddha also frowns on any miracle or revelation. He might even have made seemingly conflicting sermons to different groups with different intellectual levels for the sake of easy comprehension. At present, there are many denominations stressing different points of philosophy. To give a detailed account of the formation and development of the Buddhistic order as a religion would be very boring and also unnecessary.

In this book, we are interested in Zen Buddhism, which has kept the essence of Siddhatha Gotama's original philosophy, reinforced by Chinese Taoism, minus ceremonial rites developed in later years.

It is sufficient for us to say that Zen has probed into the hard core of human problems. It believes that if we know our view to be incorrect, and that if we know what is the correct view, then, the rest--right speech, right behavior, etc.---can be taken care of automatically. To Zen believers, the worship of image and the burning of incense are just different pedagogical devices of audio-visual aids in religious education. They are not essential. The major issue then is this: Is what we see and hear a reality?

With this issue in mind, we are now entering into a new chapter completely devoted to the discussion of reality vs. delusion in the light of modern physics.

Chapter 3

Physical Phenomenon vs Ultimate Reality

With the advancement of modern physics and technology, our concept of this world has been increasingly closer to that of Zen. What we used to consider a discrepancy between the world of appearance and that of Zen, is in fact, non-existing. This chapter will attempt to show how modern physics in general and quantum mechanics in particular have reshaped man's concept on reality.

According to Zen, this phenomenal world we live in is not real; and our sense perceptions are not reliable either. In order to make this belief more easily understood, ways and means have been devised. But they are not generally accepted by those uninitiated. Lately, modern physics and general semantics have begun to share the same fundamental concept of the universe as perceived by Zen believers.

We know that everything in this world can be divided into three forms or states; namely, the solid state, the liquid state, and the gaseous state. These states can be broken into molecules which can be broken again into further particles--atoms.

There are about 102 different atoms or elements, according to the atomic table worked out by scientists. Everything in this world is made from these 102 atoms.

Atoms can be again divided into electrons, protons, and neutrons. Electrons have negative

16

charge, protons, positive charge, and neutrons, neutral. An electron is really tiny. It has only a mass of 9.11×10^{-28} gram. The 102 atoms are different and each kind has its own property or characteristics, simply because the structure of different atoms are different. To be more specific, in different atoms, the number of electrons whirling around the nucleus is different. Therefore, what we consider to be the external physical world can be said to be nothing more than different arrangements and combinations of molecules, which are made of atoms. Atoms are made of electrons and protons.

In the solid state of matter, each molecule is confined to a definite small space between neighboring molecules. In the liquid state of matter, molecules are less tightly packed. When a substance is in the gaseous state, the molecules are still less crowded.

Modern physics has further shown us that mass is a form of energy. All forms of radiant energy in space, therefore, can congeal into particles of matter--electrons, atoms, and molecules--which may then combine to form large units, such as nebulas, stars, and ultimately galactic systems. These forms of radiant energy in space travel in separate and discontinuous quanta. Our sensation of color arises from the bombardment of our optic nerves by light quanta.

In Diagram 1, the electro-magnetic spectrum has shown us clearly that our eyes are limited in vision. We cannot see radio and television waves. We cannot see ultraviolet and infrared rays. We

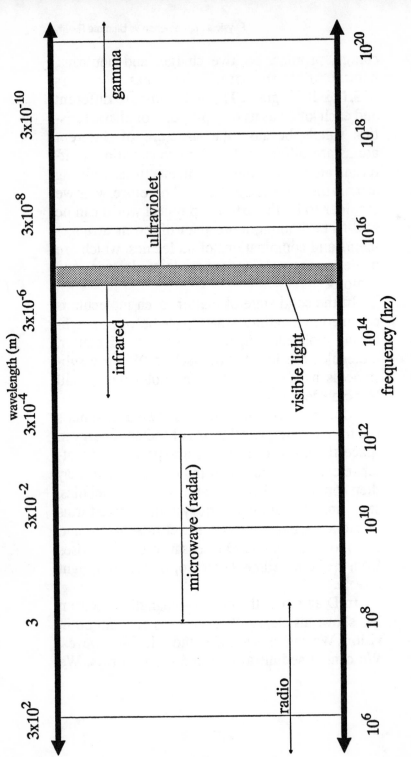

Diagram 1. The Electromagnetic Spectrum

can not see X-rays. In fact, on this wide spectrum, we can only see light rays which constitute only a fraction of the band. The rest is non-seeing, but existing. Anybody can test the existence of these radiations with proper training and instruments. It is scientific, empirical, and not imaginary.

It is also true with our ears. The range of sound waves audible to the human ear is between 20 and 16,000 vibrations per second. Beyond this range, the rest can register on instruments only. Some animals have better hearing or seeing organs than humans. This fact is quite well known.

The philosophical aspect of these recent scientific discoveries is this: Now it is established that what we see and what we hear are not the world in its entirety. With such limitations, it is almost impossible for us to visualize the actual world we live in.

So Buddha said about 2,500 years ago, "When you are viewing the whole appearance of a country, seeing its mountains, rivers, people, etc., there seems to be discriminated particulars. But in truth, they are all made up by the original, beginningless sickness of perceiving eyes".

When he spoke of the "original beginningless sickness of perceiving eyes", he meant that our seeing organs have always been defective and imperfect from the very beginning.

What has been discussed so far in this chapter is not the whole story. Ordinarily, since we do the seeing, we do not bother too much about the structure of our own apparatus of vision. Usually, we just study the intrinsic characteristics or physical properties of an object, and we take it for granted that the responding organism does not have to be taken into consideration. But in actuality, the nature of any object under examination and even its very existence have a lot to do with the responding organism. All characteristics of an object, such as color, smell, sound, texture and taste are entirely dependent upon the structure of the recipient or the organism responding to it. Without a responding organism, an object is neither existing nor non-existing.

For instance, when a color blind person looks at a colorful object, certainly, he would miss all the hues except the grey color. By the same token, if our eyes are as penetrating as X-rays, then what we can see will be entirely different from what we see now.

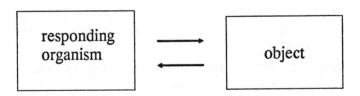

In the history of Zen, an incident was recorded somewhat like this: Once Hui Neng, the Sixth Patriarch, was going to address his congregation. Some members in the audience, after seeing a flag blown by the wind outside the hall, were arguing why the flag waved. Is it because of the wind or because the flag did so itself? Hui Neng made a remark, "It is because of your mind."

Based on this view, it is very easy to solve the following argument. If there is no person around, when a tree falls in the forest, is there any sound? Naturally there is no sound. Because sound is made from air vibrations, if sound waves are not received and interpreted by any hearing mechanism, sound waves remain as waves, and there is no sound.

In short, the nature and appearance of this world depend on who is the responding organism and what is its structure. The physical objects themselves are devoid of color, smell, sound, texture and taste.

When we human beings see an object, we have the same response. It is not because there is a mystic and abstract "universal mind" as Kant observed, but because we have similar responding organisms. Thus, we react in the same way.

In the *Diamond Sutra*, Buddha warned the truthseekers that, "Although terrestrial human beings have always grasped after the arbitrary conception of matter and great universes, the conception has no true basis--it is an illusion of the mortal mind."

Both science and Zen have proved that the phenomenal world we see is not real. While science is interested in the intrinsic nature of the physical world, Zen is primarily concerned with man and his relations with the physical world. Or rather, Zen is primarily concerned with man as one kind of responding organism with respect to nature or the external physical world. Both of them do not, however, touch the problem of creation. Where did the original mass or energy come from? This

21

basic problem will be discussed in the chapter on infinity.

In the next chapter, we have another approach to Zen -- the semantic approach. By employing this new empirical science of linguistics, we will have a fresh approach to the age-honored problems: Do we have a soul? What is the mind? In the light of modern general semantics, we can probably solve some other related problems too.

Chapter 4

The Nature of Language

Normally, we consider language as a means of communication. In our daily living, we cannot dispense with it without encountering serious difficulties. Through language, not only can we express our thoughts, we can also promote understanding. But any language, spoken or written, is a set of symbols or signs, and meanings are arbitrarily assigned to them. Since a symbol can only symbolize something and not the thing itself, and a sign can only signify something and not the thing itself, can we really express reality through language?

If language cannot express reality, what then is the relationship between language and reality? In this chapter we are going to study the symbolic nature of language with its relation to reality or the empirical world. We are going to employ general semantics as a means to clarify our doubts.

General semantics is a new science which deals with the relationship between language symbols and their corresponding objects. According to this discipline, language is a map, whereas the empirical world or reality is the territory. In order to make the map meaningful, it has to structurally correspond to the territory.

For instance, if we make a map of this country, we have to put San Francisco in the West, New York in the East, and Chicago somewhere between. If you are not familiar with the country, a map is very helpful. In fact, it is a necessity.

On the other hand, if someone put something extra on the map which is non-existing, what is going to happen? From the map alone you cannot detect anything wrong. But, when actually checking the territory, you realize the extra mark is non-existing. In case you encounter such terms in our language, that is, terms which verbally exist, but are non-existing in reality, what are you going to do? This is a very serious problem. Many philosophical and religious disagreements are, in fact, linguistic problems because they fall into this category.

We know that terms such as time and space, body and mind exist in our language. But do they really exist separately? We take for granted that since there are two different terms in our language, therefore, there must be two different items, physical or abstract, independent of each other. In actuality, this concept cannot be accepted without further scrutiny.

We understand now that space is simply a possible order of material objects; and time is simply a possible order of events. Space has no objective reality except as an order or arrangement of the objects as we perceive it. And time has no independent existence apart from the order of events by which we measure it. This time-space integration has been well demonstrated by Einstein already.

As far as the mind is concerned, many chapters have been written in psychology textbooks on this subject, and yet what is the mind is still very obscure. On the other hand, there is increasing evidence in biological science that an organism always functions as a whole. You cannot separate body from mind, and mind from body. In other words, we may verbally split body from mind, space from time, etc.; however, they can never be separated empirically.

Here is a very interesting linguistic phenomenon which can support this view. There is no such word as mind in the Chinese language. Chinese people use the character 心 pronounced as *hsin* instead. "*Hsin*" also means heart which is a physical organ and can be located easily.

On the other hand, it is possible that there is not an adequate term in our language to express a physical phenomenon newly discovered by man. For instance, light sometimes acts like waves, and sometimes has the characteristics of particles. Whether light should be considered as waves or particles has been a subject of considerable dispute. From the semantic point of view, it is very easy to explain. Prior to the advent of modern physics, man never dreamed that such a phenomenon could exist. Therefore, there is no corresponding term to designate it.

Now, in order to make a language structurally corresponding to nature, a new term denoting something with characteristics of waves and particles should be coined.

Diagram 2 is very important in general semantics. By looking at it closely, we can see the inadequacy of language. The event level in this diagram can be characterized as infinite complexity, con-

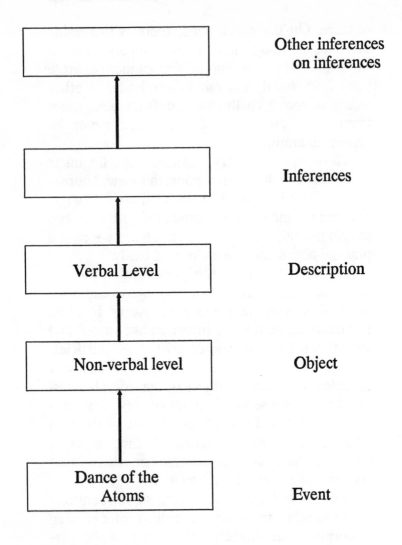

	Other inferences on inferences
Verbal Level	Inferences
Verbal Level	Description
Non-verbal level	Object
Dance of the Atoms	Event

Diagram 2. LEVELS OF ABSTRACTION

stant change, and non-identity of events. It is the level where atoms dance.

The next level is the level of objects. On this level, names have not been given to objects yet. It is a non-verbal level. Next we come to the level of description. From here on, language is used.

On this level, when we name an object, say "house", we actually can get the common denominators of a structure. Strictly speaking, no two houses are identical. When we utter a word like house, we lose a lot of characteristics peculiar to that house in the process of abstracting. For this reason, what we call a house cannot be identified with any particular house, because each house has its own characteristics.

About 2,500 years ago, Lao Tzu in China seemed to be aware of the inadequacies of language. In his book *Tao Te Ching*, (道德經) he made a negative approach to Tao, translated as "the Way" or the unknown factor governing the universe. He explained what is not Tao in his book. This book is generally considered as the Bible of Taoism. He said he could not tell people what Tao is through language. If he did, it would no longer be the Tao he conceived in his mind. In other words, the Chinese philosopher at that time was quite apprehensive of the fact that in the process of abstracting, many characteristics he associated with the word Tao would be lost. Therefore, the meaning of Tao he had in mind would never be the same as other people might have.

The next level in the diagram is the level of inference. When we infer something, that inference

27

is our own opinion or judgement. It is subjective in nature, and far from the fact. If we make another inference based on another's inference or judgement, we are even further from the objective world. This level is indicated by the first line in the diagram.

This world is complicated by the fact that everything is changing, and nothing is permanent. This world is a world of process. And it is impossible to use words verbally to identify processes.

On top of this complexity is the fact that the observer himself is not a constant. He is changing too. Under circumstances like this, what we can say is that the "object" of our experience is not the "thing in itself", but an interaction between our nervous system and something outside it. In other words, everything is a function of something else. Nothing is absolute. Nothing is definite. From this train of thought, we arrived at this conclusion:

Not only   Man 1 $\neq$ Man 2
but also   Man 1 of 1960 $\neq$ Man 1 of 1967.

Buddha's Dharma goes even one step further than general semantics in this respect. According to the Dharma, human beings are just one kind of organism or living beings in this world, and there are innumerable kinds of organisms in this world, let alone other planets. Therefore, object one of 1967 viewed by one species of organisms is not identical to the same object one of 1967 viewed by another species of organisms, since we know that all objects themselves are devoid of characteristics such as color, smell and sound. These characteristics are attributes dependent on the structurally different responding organisms.

In the history of Chinese philosophy, the Neo-Confucian school has revealed that the Great Tao or the ultimate truth is the function of our own mind. (大道即人心)

Now, let us get back to Diagram 2 and see where Zen stands in terms of Levels of Abstraction, when it looks at the phenomenal world. In the Sutra spoken by the Sixth Patriarch Hui Neng an episode was recorded by the author.

Before he became the Patriarch, Hui Neng was working in a monastery trying to learn Zen Buddhism. One day, the Fifth Patriarch summoned all of his disciples to his office, telling them that he was going to retire. He expected those interested in the position to submit their poems to him so he could evaluate their understanding of Zen and give the position to the most qualified disciple.

The head student was interested in the post but afraid that the master would not give it to him. Hence, he wrote a verse and posted it on the wall outside of the Patriarch's office anonymously, thinking that if the master did not approve of it, he still would not lose face in front of other disciples. If on the other hand, the master liked it, he would then identify the authorship. The rendition of his verse in English is somewhat like this:

Our body may be compared to the Bodhi tree,
While our mind is a mirror bright;

Constantly keep it clean,
And let no dust collect on it.

In his Sutra, Hui Neng said he was illiterate. He saw the poem but could not read. Since he was anxious to know its contents, he asked another student to read for him. After hearing the poem, he said he also had another one in mind. He requested his friend to do him a favor by writing on the wall what he had to say. The following is the translation of his dictation:

Originally, the Bodhi was not a tree,
Nor was the mind a mirror bright;
Since there wasn't a thing at first,
Where could the dust collect?

After the Fifth Patriarch discovered the two verses, the Robe and the Bowl, both symbols of authority, were transmitted to Hui Neng, according to the Sutra.

Poetry is a metric language. It is almost impossible to translate a poem from one language to another without losing some rhyme, rhythm, imagery, and beauty of the original text. For our purpose, let us ignore the aesthetic aspect of the translated verses, but analyze the meaning of each one. And let us examine critically these two verses in the light of modern general semantics.

Under normal circumstances, the first poem should be considered a good poem. The author used metaphorical language to illustrate a point. He compared our body to a bodhi tree and our

30

mind to a reflecting mirror. Since Buddha was en-lightened under a bodhi tree, to mention that tree in the poem is quite appropriate. The name bodhi here makes us associate with Buddha's Dharma and his enlightenment.

The author was trying to convey the idea in the poem that if we keep our mind serene, undis-turbed, and detached, just as we keep our mirror clean and bright, then whatever is reflected on our mind will be just whatever is reflected on a mirror- -- a perfect image. There is no distortion what-soever.

In other words, if we keep our mind clear, we can see everything as it is. We can probably see not only the appearance but also the nature of every-thing in our mind's eye. In poetry, metaphors are usually employed and accepted. In this poem, the author was speaking on the descriptive level in the Levels of Abstraction.

In the second poem, the author refuted the comparison, body as bodhi tree, mind as mirror, on the ground that at the very beginning there was no body, no tree, no mind, no mirror, and no dust. Everything was undifferentiated. The author was talking on the bottom level in the Levels of Abstraction. Zen is always aiming at this basic level. According to Buddha's pristine Dharma, the phenomenal reality is not the ultimate reality, be-cause it is on the descriptive level of abstraction. It is always perceived differently by different kinds of responding organisms. It lacks the quality of universality and permanency. We cannot and should not accept that whatever one kind of responding organism perceives is the final and only reality. Buddhism is very firm on this view. There is no compromise.

It may be conceded, however, that the phenomenal world is true and real as one particular species of responding organisms are concerned at a certain moment, since they have the same make-up and they may have the same response to the same outside stimuli.

In order to get to the ultimate in everything, we have to come to the bottom level of Abstraction, before things are differentiated. Wordsworth, the 19th century British poet, once expressed his philosophy in these words: "We do not die, we only change." He was then talking on the same level of abstraction as Zen.

On the other hand, when Lao Tzu made this statement, "Whenever there is life, there is death", we must understand that he was speaking on the descriptive level in the Level of Abstraction.

Finally, general semantics probably can clarify one more major point in Buddhism, the misconception of Nirvana. Nirvana is the ultimate goal of all Buddhists. The popular belief is that Nirvana is a place where they go after this life. It is the place where they can enjoy themselves forever.

According to the Hinayana school, Nirvana means extinction of illusion. According to the Mahayana school, Nirvana means attainment of truth. In any event, Nirvana is not a place; it is a state of mind. There is no outside referent for the term Nirvana other than what you conceive in your own mind. If a person is said to have crossed to the other shore and attained Nirvana, that means he has fathomed the profound truth taught by Buddha. He is enlightened. To cross the river and to attain Nirvana are two metaphors. They should not be viewed literally.

Chapter 5

The Theory of Equilibrium

Zen, though proven to be correct as far as man's reasoning power goes, is sometimes criticized for being outwardly. Its indifference to the material progress of the human race has caused much concern. Many people, especially people from the West, do not agree with such an attitude.

Fortunately, in China, such indifference is counteracted by Confucius' philosophy on human relations. An individual should be responsible to himself, his family, his country, and the entire world. Its ultimate aim is to create a world of peace, order, and justice on earth. Chinese intellectual history revolves around the framework of Confucius' teaching.

This chapter is going to elucidate a theory which will enable us to see the proper place of Zen's role in human society. This theory owes its existence to modern physics as well as Confucius' doctrine of the golden mean. When tested, it seems to underlie all events both natural and human. This author calls it the theory of equilibrium. Its universality demands our close examination.

In modern physics, the fundamental particles in the structure of any atom are the negatively charged electrons, the positively charged protons and the neutrons, which are neutral. If the electrons and protons are not equal in number, in other words, if they are not balanced, then the atom in question will change into an ion. It may release energy in order to keep the atom in a new balanced state. Thus equilibrium is maintained when these two forces or energies are balanced.

On the other hand, Confucius did, in effect, put such a concept of equilibrium in his teaching when applied to human relations. It is known as the doctrine of the golden mean. According to his teaching, when we pilot our course in human affairs, we should always take the middle way. We should avoid extremism. We should be moderate.

Of course, there is a difference between equilibrium and moderation. Equilibrium refers to a state of balance between opposing forces or actions, whereas moderation means to keep within due bounds or observe reasonable limits, or to be calm, temperate, and exercise restraint. In case of conflict, we should solve the problem through mediation rather than resort to violence.

In biology, the self-regulating process of living organisms is called homeostasis. When we have excessive heat in our body, our skin pores will automatically open up and let the excessive heat inside evaporate until our body temperature lowers to its normal level.

In thermo-dynamics, the feedback system can be engineered to work. Home appliances like automatic heaters and hot water tanks are equipped with such devices. If you set a certain temperature, the mechanism will forever seek and adjust around such a desired degree. Thus, the machine will work and regulate itself at the same time.

From the observation mentioned above, it seems that when a thing is at rest, it is not really static. It is merely a condition where two or more composite forces are in balance. Or it will not stand as it is. It will change until a new equilibrium is attained. In other words, anything in order or at rest is a state in which two or more opposing forces are in equilibrium.

This theory can apply from the simplest atom to complicated living organisms and man-made machines. It can apply to the mechanisms in human relations too. The validity of this theory can be witnessed also by the following human disciplines.

In Education

In education, the present controversy over general education versus specialization should be stated in terms of equilibrium. In our age, a highly educated person specialized in one subject generally ignores the rest not under research. As a result of this over specialization, laws and principles generalized by him will fit only one set of events. They will not have universal application. It is therefore important for those who specialize in science or other professions to have adequate knowledge of some disciplines other than their own. The purpose is to broaden their horizons and let them see where they stand in the overall picture. After all, knowledge means order or structure. It is not merely acquisition of some technical terms.

In Government

In the history of political thought, various forms of government have been illustrated. It seems to be that if it is the government of the people and if it wants to function better and last longer, it must fulfill the following requirements.

It must have two major political parties competing with each other. In this way, each party is forever incorporating wishes of the people into its platforms, hoping that it can win the next election.

In order to prevent power from being concentrated in one person or one agency, a system of division of power--checks and balances--must be devised. The problem of centralization and decentralization of power between the national government and local governments should also be carefully weighed and balanced.

Under such a political system, regardless of its name, if its practices agree with the theory of equilibrium, it will not disintegrate easily.

In Diet

The composition of our diet must be balanced. To be overdosed with one component is just as bad as to be under-dosed. If we take one type of vitamin in excess as food supplement, it may even be poisonous. We need other vitamins to neutralize it. This is another example of the law of equilibrium at work.

In short, equilibrium is the state of optimum adjustment where opposing forces or actions are stabilized. To seek optimum adjustment is a natural phenomenon, and the mechanism to perform it is inherent in everything.

In this world everything is dynamic. And our life is many sided. To pilot a course of the golden mean in our life's journey is not a small matter. Let us just take one aspect to illustrate the difficulties involved. If we want to be healthy, not only must we balance our diet, we must have sufficient physical exercise and rest to compliment the diet. And of course, exercise and rest themselves have to be balanced too.

But to have a balanced diet, exercise, and rest alone does not make us healthy. Our state of mind has to be taken into consideration. We have to pay attention to mental hygiene as well. We know too well that excessive worry will affect our physical health. Some doctors have remarked that man's life span should be longer than what current statistics indicate. But man does not live as long as he should, because he does not live under optimum conditions.

Since the mechanism to attain equilibrium is inherent in our body, that is why after we have lived in one environment we yearn for another one. City dwellers like to go to the countryside to enjoy fresh air, open space, and serenity. Country folk like to visit cities to enjoy the crowds, the bustling and to become a part of the fast moving tempo of humanity. After a trip usually we can work better.

Since the mechanism to attain equilibrium is inherent in our body, that is also why in modern society, assembly line work, where only one set of muscles is used with little or no thinking at all, proves to be boring and monotonous.

These examples indicate that varied activities and occasional change of environment can promote our physical and mental health, and make life more interesting. To live in accordance with the law of equilibrium means to know the secret of science and the art of living.

Now, let us move to larger units and see how equilibrium works. Man by nature is an aggregate animal. He cannot live alone. He has to aggregate in order to live. More problems arise from this aggregate nature of man. Otherwise, life's problems would be much simpler. In fact, we devote most of our time and energy to solve human problems on different levels and in different aspects. Political, military, economic and social problems are exacting. They have taxed much of our ingenuity. While engaged in solving those problems, sometimes, we forget ourselves. Aristotle's remark, "To know thyself" remains a good warning to us busy modern men.

In order to balance our one-sided worldliness, naturally, Zen comes into the picture. Buddha designated his course of action as the middle way. He did not believe in asceticism as a means to attain enlightenment, nor did he believe in Brahman worship as a way of salvation. In other words, Zen itself is balanced.

However, we, the average people, are the bulk of the human race. While believing in the teaching of Zen, we must not neglect our duty as a member of human society. If everyone follows Buddha's prescribed Dharma closely and lives as hermits or monks, the human race itself will soon come to an end.

On the other hand, since it is humanly impossible to have all desires materialized, we are bound to have disappointments and dissatisfactions in life. When a crisis arises, we can always find solace, comfort, and courage in Zen. In our daily meditation we can also find inner peace and joy. After meditation, we can regain our lost perspective in life and feel much clearer in thinking, which will help us a great deal when we pilot our course in human relations and make optimum adjustments in worldly affairs.

Thus, the law of equilibrium seems to be always in operation, from the smallest unit of the atom to the largest divisions of human activities. It bridges the gap between physical sciences on one hand, and social sciences on the other. Can we then venture to say that equilibrium is the fifth dimension, even if it lacks the quality of extent, as length, breadth, depth, and time?

Chapter 6

The Anatomy of Happiness

What is Happiness?

The United States Declaration of Independence says among many other things that all men are created equal, that they are endowed by their creator with certain inalienable rights, that among these are life, liberty, and the pursuit of happiness. Pursuit of happiness, then, is and should be our supreme goal in life.

What is happiness then? Many people are confused with the two terms, happiness and pleasure. While they are seeking pleasure, they think they just want to be happy. Happiness is different from pleasure. Happiness comes from within. It is a state of mind. If you are content, you are happy.

Pleasure denotes sensuous gratification. It comes from outside. If you want to use liquor as a kind of stimuli or a means to console yourself, you may get temporary relief from the drinks because liquor does have a sedative effect on your nerves. But the very next day, contrary to what you expect, you have misery instead of happiness.

Can cigarette smoking give you happiness? Statistics show that there is a link between cigarette smoking and lung cancer. No wonder tobacco companies always advertise that their products generated smoking pleasure. They dare not use the term "smoking happiness" to allure people, because there is no happiness in smoking.

41

Besides, both drinking and smoking are acquired habits. They are not innate in man. You do not have to be addicted to these habits as prerequisites for happiness.

Happiness is closely related to desire. The more desire you have, the less happy you become. In modern times, many desires are created by advertisers. They use prestige or social status to promote their products which are already being used by the public, but which are not basic items necessary to sustain life. Sometimes, they even try to create the image that using their new products is a symbol of prestige or status. Actually, never before in the history of mankind did these new products have anything to do with our social standing. Since we are constantly bombarded by these commercials through the mass media, we are likely to be susceptible to their subtle suggestions. And before long, we become their prey. If we do not purchase what they want us to purchase, we feel unhappy.

Happiness is a very subjective thing. We cannot use outside objective achievement to measure happiness within. Chuang Tzu, the disciple of Lao Tzu, illustrated this point very well in the chapter "Nan Hwa Ching". He said that once there were a big bird and a little insect. Both of them searched for happiness. Finally, the bird discovered that once in awhile it must migrate to a far away place in order to be happy. This creature found immense happiness in its flight in boundless space. The little insect also discovered that in order to be happy, it must hop a few inches. In its little hop, the insect had full expression of its personality; and there-fore, found its supreme happiness therein.

If we measure happiness in terms of distances one can cover--say, the longer the distance, the bigger the happiness-- then, long before the insect got to the bird's destination, the little creature would perish. From this story we can see that while we might compare ourselves with others, we should always take our own capabilities into consideration.

Another characteristic feature of happiness is that you cannot buy happiness with money. Your happiness is not necessarily in proportion to the amount of money you possess. This statement might just be opposite to what people generally believe. Before we debate on the validity of this statement, let us first examine what money is.

In a modern society, money seems to be very important in life. With money, we think we can buy whatever we like. As a matter of fact, our work is paid by money. To most people, a person's success in life is measured in terms of the money he can make. The more money he can make, the greater is his success in life. Looking at it this way, money seems to have a direct bearing on one's well-being.

This being the case, why then are wealthy men not always happy. Some cannot solve life's problems. They have to resort to committing suicide. While living, they must compute their income taxes and inheritance taxes carefully in order to save money. But when they leave this world, they still cannot take away with them their hard earned money. This is the most tragic part of the whole money-making story.

Now, let us scrutinize money a little further and see whether it deserves so much of our attention or not. It is true that money has purchasing power. We can use money to purchase commodities and pay for services. Money, therefore, can be defined as a means of exchange. We cannot get along without money in a modern society.

Can we, however, buy something from savages, and expect them to accept our money for payment? Certainly not. To them, paper money has no value whatsoever. Again, if we know that the paper money now in circulation does not have any backing or reserve, do you think we will trust it or consider it to have any value? Certainly not. In the final analysis, money then is just a contract. So long as all the parties concerned honor the contract, it works. We pass it over from one hand to the other, assuming that it has purchasing power. If we assume that it has purchasing power, then it automatically has magic power among us honoring it. Otherwise, it is just a piece of paper. There is no intrinsic value in it.

In short, the functional value of any monetary system depends on the faith or trust of the people concerned. It is psychological in nature. We should, therefore, dismiss this erroneous concept that money itself is almighty.

Since happiness cannot be bought with money and since happiness is a state of mind, every one of us, thus, can be potentially happy. As a matter of fact, happiness is always with us. The problem is how to discover it by removing those countless unnecessary desires. Buddha's Dharma, discussed in previous chapters and in the next few chapters, will serve as the best technique available for self-realization of perfect happiness and eternal truth.

Chapter 7

The Existence of God

The major objectives of Buddhism are to get away from human suffering and to realize eternity or Nirvana. Ways and means have been employed to prove that the phenomenal world as we see it is not ultimate reality. But, in all Buddhistic sutras, there is a complete silence on the name of God. This fact is very significant. This conspicuous absence of God coincides with Chinese religions.

Of course, Chinese people traditionally believe in the concept that Heaven is the creator and father, and earth is the mother. This concept precedes organized religion in China.

But, Confucius said, "When you worship God (shen 神), worship as if God is there." 〔敬神如神在〕

In other words, he did not say definitely whether God exists or not.

Concerning after-life, Confucius made this statement, "We do not know life yet, how can we know death or after-life?" 〔未知生，焉知死〕

In order to show that he was not enthused with the supernatural, Confucius declared, "While respecting spirits and goblins, keep away from them." 〔敬鬼神而遠之〕

Lao Tzu, the founder of Taoism, also shared the same feeling with Confucius in this respect. He advocated no-assertion or inaction (*wu wei* 無為) in his philosophy. He advised people to be in har-

46

mony with nature. In his work *Tao Te Ching*, he never mentioned the name of God either. His no-assertion or *wu wei* philosophy has a striking similarity with the ultimate aim of Zen.

In Diagram 3, which was remodeled after the pattern of Levels of Abstraction in general semantics, the difference between science and religion on one hand and the difference among different religions on the other can be easily visualized. This writer calls it Levels of Evolution.

Historically, all major religions of the world originated in Asia. Some stressed God, creation and revelation. Some terminated at infinity. Some had nothing to do with God or nature.

Confucianism is primarily concerned with human relations, such as relations between the leader and the people, husband and wife, father and son, brothers and friends. The ultimate goal is to build a world of peace and order.

Taoism is interested in Tao, the way that the universe operates. Taoists are anxious to find out how to live in harmony with nature, and thus to prolong our life span. They did not touch the bottom level, the level of creation.

Zen, in the same manner, explains the basic components of man, and his relations with nature. It does not account for the area of creation.

Science explores and interprets the physical world. But scientists never inquire into the origin of matter. They consider this area is not the province of their inquiry. They leave it to religion and philosophy.

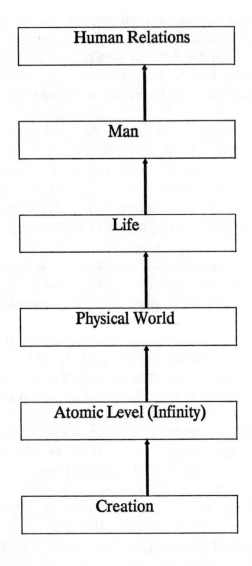

Diagram 3. LEVELS OF EVOLUTION

The difference between science and Zen is that scientists study the physical world objectively, and they assume that in everything there are characteristic features which are independent of the human observer, whereas Zen studies the physical world or phenomenal world with the apprehension that the characteristic features of everything is entirely dependent upon the observer.

According to Zen, the phenomenal world is valid only so long as the structures of the observers are the same. It is real only provided the observers and the observed both do not change. Characteristics of material objects do change with the change of the observer's structure. Therefore, what we consider to be true and real is only the function of our own structure. This phenomenal reality is not the ultimate one.

Science studies the physical world including the law of conservation of energy. But, where did the original energy come from? Where did the atoms, the building blocks of the universe, come from? Who created them? To any inquiring mind, such absence of explanation is by no means satisfactory.

In the meantime, some other religions seem to have fulfilled this basic and universal need by stressing the fundamental level, the level of creation. Since it is humanly impossible to fathom the act of creation, they rely on revelation and miracle for their assertion. We understand and appreciate their position.

The drawback of this approach to the origin of the universe is that since revelation and miracle cannot be checked and substantiated by others, it is not easy to convince people about its validity. And furthermore, history has shown that every now and then there is a new revelation. Each revelation claims to be authentic. It is too much to ask believers in one revelation to believe in another revelation. This mutually exclusive attitude usually generates conflict instead of love. And love, as a rule, is a foundation of all religious teachings. This mutually exclusive attitude creates hostility, which is exactly what the founders of those religions do not want.

By comparison, Chinese religions do not have this problem. Confucianism is basically a code of ethics. It deals with human conduct. It has served as a philosophical foundation of Chinese education. There is no conflict between Confucian teachings and other religions.

The quest for ultimate reality and eternal truth by Zen, on the other hand, terminates at infinity, which, by definition, can never reach the border, if there is any. Its teachings can be questioned and answered like any branch of knowledge. They are free from dogmatism and can be easily agreed with by any observers with the same organic make-up.

Even if Zen does not get down to the bottom of creation, it does serve many practical purposes. Through Zen, man can attain happiness individually. Through Zen, man can promote peace and understanding collectively because of its teachings of compassion and reverence for life. The operational value of Zen, therefore, should be reassessed in this space age.

Chapter 8

Do We Have a Soul?

In Chapter 4, The Nature of Language, attention was directed to the fact that in our language, some linguistic terms we use frequently are non-existing in reality. Does this word "soul" belong to this category? This chapter attempts to explain Buddha's view on this highly controversial subject in the light of modern general semantics.

According to Buddha, each individual human being is an aggregate of the following components, namely:

1. Body
2. Sensation
3. Thought
4. Disposition
5. Understanding.

The union of these five parts constitute the individual. At death, the union is dissolved, and the aggregation dispersed. What is called the soul or ego is, therefore, but the name we give to the functional unity which subsists when the five components constitute an individual.

Buddha seemed to doubt the existence of soul substance. According to him, in the transmigration of soul, rebirth takes place without any actual soul substance passing over from one existence to another. He explained reincarnation this way: When reincarnation takes place, it is like a seal

51

pressed upon wax. Only the characters engraved on the seal are to be retained by the wax. The seal itself does not pass over to the next existence.

Do you remember some verses you learned when you were young? Did those verses pass over (or transmigrate) to you from your teacher and he himself does not retain those verses any more? No, certainly, it is not the case.

The relationship between body and soul can be illustrated by another analogy. When a person speaks well, he can capture the attention of his audience. He is said to have a good personality. Or we say that he speaks with an air of authority. But as soon as he ceases talking, where is his personality or the air of authority?

Buddha's revolutionary concept on soul existence probably was the major reason why Buddhism was not generally accepted in its native soil, India. But general semantics can shed more light on this controversial issue than any other discipline in previous times. Semantically speaking, the problem of the existence of a soul is basically not a theological problem. It is a linguistic problem. The hard core of the problem is this: Does the word "soul" coined by man have a referent in reality? Can we split body from soul empirically? Or is soul just a functional appearance of a living organism, such as personality of an individual? Or does it just refer to something that does not have any substance of its own?

Since soul substance cannot be isolated, captured, or tested after an individual's death, general semantics can not but support Buddha's view on this issue.

Chapter 9

What is Nirvana? ---A Semantic View

Nirvana is the ultimate goal of Buddhistic devotion. What is Nirvana then? Is it a place where one can enjoy everlasting happiness? If it is, where is it? From the view point of modern general semantics, is there really a thing called Nirvana? Or is it just a name that does not have any cor- responding referent? These questions will be dis- cussed in this chapter.

First, let us quote what Buddha had to say on this vital subject. The following passage is taken from the *Lankavatara Scripture*, a lecture delivered by Buddha himself about 2,500 years ago.

The Tathagata's Nirvana (Tathagata is 如來 *Ru Lai* in Chinese, meaning the perfect one) is where it is recognized that there is nothing but what is seen by the mind itself; where, recognizing the nature of the self mind, one no longer cherishes the duelists of discrimination; where there is no more thirst for grasping; where there is no more at- tachment to external things. It is where the think- ing mind with all its discriminations, attachments, aversions, and egoism is forever put away; . . . where even the notion of truth is treated with in- difference because of its causing bewilderment; .. . where compassion for others transcends all thoughts of self.

53

The root "va" in Nirvana means to blow, and the prefix "nir" means off or out in Sanskrit. Nirvana, therefore, means the blowing out, i.e. the blowing out of the flame of personal desire in Sanskrit.

Hence, Nirvana is not a place. It is a state of mind, an attitude in looking at the phenomenal world. In other words, when your mind is in a state of perfect freedom, and all disturbances such as passion, hatred and delusion have vanished forever, you have attained Nirvana.

Nagarjuna in the second century A.D. analyzed the nature of Nirvana in this way according to his "Examination of Nirvana":

IV.

Nirvana, first of all, is not a kind of Being,
It would then have decay and death.
There altogether is no Being
Which is not subject to decay and death.

VIII.

Now, if Nirvana is a non-Being,
How can it then be independent?
For sure, an independent non-Being
is no where to be found.

XVI.

If Nirvana is neither Being nor non-Being
No one can really understand
This doctrine which proclaims at once
Negation of them both together.

After his exhaustive examination of nirvana, Nagarjuna finally concluded that:

Bliss consists in the cessation of all thought,
In the quiescence of plurality.
No separate reality was preached at all,
Nowhere and none by Buddha!

The most interesting area in the concept of Nirvana is its linkage between the attainment of Nirvana and the compassion for others. "So long as other beings do not attain Nirvana, I will not attain it myself." This is the vow every devotee must first pledge before he seriously contemplates entering into the order.

Since alleviation of human suffering is the basic concern of Buddhism, it is quite natural for Mahayana Buddhists to develop their self-sacrificing philosophy that a devotee must extend his helping hand to whomever is needed. Such a selfless and noble idea has given inspiration and courage to those needed for salvation. Such public service minded philosophy is probably the most urgently needed philosophy in this world.

Since saving others has the priority over saving oneself, and since there is always suffering so long as there is life, the founder of this great religion declared that for Buddhas there is no Nirvana.

PART II

THE DHARMA AND ITS APPLICATION

Chapter 10

Meditation: The Exploration of Inner Space

Since Zen means Dhyana and Dhyana means meditation, to talk about Zen without mentioning meditation seems to have missed the essential part of this school. This chapter, therefore, will be devoted entirely to meditation. This author will not attempt to present his views on such a vital subject. Instead, he will quote extensively what Hui Neng, the founder of this meditation school had to say on the subject.

The primary objective of meditation is to seek supreme attainment or realization of Nirvana. The first phase of meditation is concentration. To be able to concentrate is a prerequisite to meditation. We can concentrate on anything, tangible or intangible. But it is preferable to concentrate on some ideas such as love, peace, or eternity.

The power of concentration is tremendous. It is a well known fact that when we are under the sunshine, we only feel the warmth of the sun. If, on the other hand, we use a concave lens and let the sun's rays concentrate on one point, they can even make the paper burn.

The following are just a few examples to show the power of concentration.

ESP (Extra sensory perception)

59

Extra sensory perception is a mysterious and exciting subject people often speak about. From the point of view of meditation, thought transference, mind reading, clairvoyance, any extra perception is possible. In some universities in the United States, research on ESP is being conducted. It is called parapsychology. One article published in the 1967, issue of Popular Electronics also reported that the Soviet Union is interested in the subject of ESP. It is called biological radio.

According to modern science, the exact function of certain portions in our brain are still unknown. Therefore, it is possible that our brain can function as a radio broadcasting station as well as a radio receiving set. If we concentrate our attention on certain matter and beam at certain persons, radio waves of certain length can be sent out. If another person can tune in, he can pick up the message. Experiments have been made that our brain can produce enough electrical current to make an electric bulb flash.

Treatment of Illness

Our sickness may be grouped into two categories, namely, physical and mental. The recent development in psychosomatic medicine has clearly demonstrated the intimate relations between body and mind. In other words, our body can affect our mind, and our mind can affect our body. For instance, when you were eating, suddenly, you learned that someone in your family has had an accident. Right away, your stomach would stop producing the acid necessary for digestion, and consequently, you would no longer have any appetite. Conversely, if you were sick and your beloved one who was in a faraway place, unexpectedly came to see you, you would feel much better not only mentally but also physically.

Many physical symptoms of our illnesses have mental origins. Our aches and pains may be due to tension, worry or frustration. If that is the case, the best remedy is to practice "stopping" or "insight". Stopping means to remove undesirable conditions and habits. Insight means to examine critically the phenomenal world we live in and to try realizing its emptiness. If we keep on scrutinizing this phenomenal world, our thoughts will be more penetrating. Our body will be serene. We will feel calm even if we are confronted with what ordinarily is considered an insurmountable problem. Of course, we will seek a solution to the problem. But we will not get emotional, excited or frustrated. We will solve the problem objectively under any circumstances. The solution thus made would be better than any other avenue of approach. People interested in the field of mental hygiene should, therefore, investigate more the principles and techniques of meditation as a form of therapy.

It is also known that some people well versed in the technique of meditation can cure another person's sickness by touching, and sometimes not even touching the uncomfortable area. They work on the theory that there is *ch'i* (prana) in the air. *Ch'i* is the life sustaining element in the air. It is not exactly a chemical component of the air we inhale. By controlled breathing, we get more *ch'i*. If we transfer the extra ch'i to another person, it has curing effect. Such technique has been reported in the literature dealing with this subject. But caution should be made here that this is not for amateurs. If not done properly, adverse effects can be produced on the part of the healer.

Meditation of the Neo-Confucian school in China has a moral implication. The practitioners claim that if we sit alone in a quiet environment, the meditative mood can provide us with an opportunity to introspect ourselves. These solitary moments can capture what our active life usually misses--an opportunity to examine our past and to outline a guide for the future. A moment of silence can make us think twice about what we should do and what we should not do toward our fellow men. It is often the case that the greatest moments in our life are the moments we are alone. Because these are the times vital decisions in our life are being made.

Poets and philosophers are always thinking. Sometimes, they are not understood by their contemporaries. When they think deeply, their power of observation is keen and their reasoning faculty is sharp. They can penetrate the surface of the phenomenal world and unearth the hidden truth. No wonder they are ahead of their times and it is not easy for others to understand them.

Extra sensory perception and the treatment of the sick are just the ramifications of meditation. A true Zen devotee should go much further than these and not be sidetracked by its supernatural power.

In the tradition of Chinese meditation school, there are three things which are very important in the practice of Dhyana:

1. Non-objectivity as basis: （ 無相爲體）

We should not be absorbed in objects when we are in contact with objects. We should free ourselves from dependence upon externals.

2. Idea-lessness as object: （ 無念爲宗）

We should not be carried away by any idea in our exercise of the mental faculty. We should keep our mind free from defilement under all circumstances.

3. Non-attachment as principle: （無住爲本）

We should not cherish any desire for or aversion to any particular thing or idea. To dwell on the succession of ideas will give rise to bondage. If we let our mind become detached at any time to anything, we gain emancipation.

In the *Sutra Spoken by the Sixth Patriarch* (六 祖法寶壇經）, Hui Neng said Dhyana means first to gain freedom of mind and to be entirely unperturbed under all outward circumstances, be they good or otherwise.

The difference between Dhyana (meditation) and Samadhi (absorbed contemplation or trance) is this:

"Dhyana is the effort to be mentally free from any attachment to outer objects. Samadhi is the

63

realization of that freedom in inward peace." In other words, "to be free from attachment is Dhyana, and to realize inner peace is Samadhi. At the very moment that Samadhi is realized, Prajna (insight, 慧) is attained."

Please notice here the ultimate goal of Zen has a striking similarity with the Taoist philosophy, the philosophy of no-assertion. It is therefore, safe to say that Chinese Taoism did play an important role in shaping the form and content of Hui Neng's meditation school.

Chapter 11

Buddhistic Compassion

Buddhism in general and the Mahayana school of Buddhism in particular stress the concept of compassion. According to the Mahayana school, a devotee interested in entering Nirvana must first make a pledge that even if he is qualified, he will not enter unless and until he has saved all suffering humanity.

Such a noble and self-imposed burden thus transmutes self-love to universal love. It translates the concept of oneness of mankind into reality. Such a compassionate attitude towards others is very inspiring. It makes people in general more optimistic, because now they can count on somebody advanced in the path for guidance and salvation.

Instead of individualism and pessimism which might be deduced from original Buddhism, Mahayana thought ushered in a new phase of philosophical development wherein Buddhism not only gives people personal satisfaction, it also furnishes the needed theoretical basis for people helping one another. It not only makes people more civic minded and less individualistic, it also makes people more self-sacrificing and less self-centered. It not only creates more hope and optimism to millions of people, it also generates more enthusiasm for the concept of egolessness and selflessness. To foster such a noble idea to help others is the greatness of Buddhism.

Absence of Sin

In any Buddhistic Sutra, the word "sin" is absent. This conspicuous absence of sin is significant. It is another illustration of Buddhistic compassion.

If a person did anything wrong morally, he is not considered a bad person or a sinner. He did it because he was ignorant. He did it because he did not know any better. Therefore, Buddha felt sorry for him. What he needs most is guidance rather than punishment. What he needs is somebody to show him a better way, the way that will not have undesirable repercussions. Such an attitude of compassion permeates all of Buddhas's lectures.

Reverence for Life

Anybody who wants to seek personal salvation must first observe this regulation--no killing. Here, "thou shalt not kill" is not so much a commandment of God. Such ruling stems from the basic tenet of Buddhistic belief--how to get away from suffering. If we want to be happy, why should we inflict suffering upon other satient beings by killing? This sensible reasoning is very easy for the average man to understand.

In the present world, where fighting and killing seem to be the only way to solve problems, Buddha's reverence for life plays a very important role in preserving human dignity and human rights. It serves as a philosophical foundation for us in search of peace.

The Concept of Karma and Crime Prevention

The Buddhistic regulation concerning one's conduct in life is very strict. Every devotee should observe the following:

1. not to kill,
2. not to steal,
3. no adultery,
4. eat the right food,
5. have the right occupation.

Buddhists believe that whatever you do your karmic deeds will remain there. "We reap what we sow, and our future is the product of our present." Such concept can make people aware of what they are doing and what they are going to do. It can supplement the deficiency of law, since law deals with an individual's external acts. It cannot regulate his intention or motivation. Buddhistic law or Karma, however, can send a warning signal to those at a time before they break the law. Therefore, in a society where people believe in the law of Karma, the problem of crime is not a serious issue. Hence, this crime prevention device of Buddhism should not be overlooked.

Conclusion

If we practice oneness of mankind instead of egotism, compassion instead of animosity, tolerance instead of violence, as taught by Buddha, then this world would be a world of peace and happiness, a world where it would be ideal to work, to live and to enjoy.

Chapter 12

Non-Aristotelian Logic

Our logical reasoning, generally speaking, is in the form of syllogisms which was formulated by the Greek philosopher Aristotle. This syllogism of inductive reasoning has a major premise, a minor premise and a conclusion. It is very useful for us to employ this device to push our frontier of knowledge forward.

But, unfortunately, this Aristotelian logic is not adequate in dealing with problems beyond this phenomenal world of dualism and relativity. Just like in physics, Newton's laws are valid only within a certain environment. Beyond that they do not work. In Euclidean geometry, there are 180 degrees in a triangle and the shortest distance between two points is a straight line connecting the two points. But non-Euclidean geometry has established that these statements are not always valid.

It is the same with Aristotle's syllogisms of inductive reasoning. They are very useful and practical in dealing with the problems on a phenomenal level, but when confronted with things undifferentiated on the atomic level, their application is very doubtful. This writer believes there is a new logical system to handle the situation, and he calls it non-Aristotelian logic.

Aristotelian logic can be classified as vertical thinking, whereas non-Aristotelian logic can be classified as lateral thinking. Lateral thinking may be considered to be eccentric and illogical compared with Aristotle's pattern of thinking. It may employ an analogy, a gesture, a sound, a laugh or a pause to explain a point. As a rule, the language used will be brief and terse.

The employment of non-Aristotelian logic as a pedagogical device for self-realization dates back to about 700 A.D.,when Zen masters tried to instruct the novices in sudden enlightenment. Since Zen masters were quite aware of the fact that the more we use our language to explain the truth, the further we are away from it. Therefore, they tried to avoid prolonged verbal discourse, and would rather resort to what the average people would call unorthodox and eccentric ways of instruction. Such methods started in China and are therefore strictly of Chinese origin.

Lateral thinking can deepen our insight into human nature. In the absence of physical science and general semantics, it can make us attain sudden enlightenment much easier. That is why Zen masters in China used to give their disciples a shock treatment whenever the latter were still trapped in the system of vertical thinking such as dwelling on two-valued orientation instead of multi-valued orientation, or thinking of the dichotomy of subject and object instead of realizing that oneness can never be analyzed.

In Zen dialogue, the master always spoke on the level where everything is undifferentiated. The value judgement which may be valid on the level of the phenomenal world cannot apply. Thus, the dialogue may be unintelligent to the average man, because they speak on different levels of abstraction or because there is a confusion of levels of abstraction.

Of course, Zen masters knew quite well that in this phenomenal world, the phenomena we see should only be treated as they are. This "suchness" is just the apparent truth and not the ultimate truth. No language can ever express that ultimate truth. Hence, enlightenment can never be taught. It is a matter of self-realization.

They believe that by a stroke of lateral thinking, the disciples could ignite their own inner light, dispel the darkness of ignorance, and gain sudden enlightenment.

Hui Neng, the Chinese Sixth Patriarch declared that prajna (wisdom) is samadhi (absorbed contemplation). Such a pronouncement is considered to be his major contribution to Buddhistic philosophy in its later development. This writer is inclined to continue with Hui Neng's trend of thought by making a bold assumption that there is a close relationship between prajna and lateral thinking. Because as soon as we use lateral thinking, we possess prajna. Therefore, this writer would venture to equate lateral thinking with prajna; namely, prajna is lateral thinking, and lateral thinking is prajna. In other words, lateral thinking, prajna, and samadhi are one and the same. Here are a few good examples:

Case History 1
There Is No Merit and Nothing is Holy

Buddhidharma, the twenty-eighth patriarch in India and the first in China, was given an audience by Emperor Wu of the Liang Dynasty in 520 A.D.

The emperor said, "I have built so many temples and monasteries; I have copied so many sacred books of Buddha; I have converted so many people; now, what merit does your reverence think I have thus accumulated?"

Buddhidharma replied, "Your majesty, no merit whatsoever."

The emperor asked, "What is considered by your reverence to be the first principle of the Holy Doctrine?"

Buddhidharma answered, "Vast emptiness, and nothing holy therein."

In this case, while the emperor was still dwelling on the level of this phenomenal world, Buddhidharma was on the atomic level. On this atomic level, naturally, there is no value judgement, no merit or demerit, nothing holy therein.

Case History 2
The Dichotomy of Subject and Object

Question: "What is the way?" a master was questioned by a curious monk.

Answer: "It is right before your eyes," said the master.

Question: "Why can't I see it myself?"

Answer: "Because you are thinking of yourself."

Question: "How about you? Do you see it?"

Answer: "So long as you see double, such as 'I don't' and 'you do', etc., your eyes are clouded."

71

Question: "When there is neither 'I' nor 'you' can one see it?"

Answer: "When there is neither 'I' nor 'you', who wants to see it?"

In other words, we are always entangled in the dichotomy of subject and object. But the ultimate reality is the oneness of everything. This oneness cannot be analyzed. This concept of oneness plays a major role in Buddhistic philosophy.

Case History 3
I Have Heard Sound Without Sound

A young monk wanted to be given a problem to ponder. So he came to see his master.

"Show me sound by clapping your two hands," said the master.

The monk clapped his hands.

"Good," said the master. "Now, show me sound by clapping one hand."

Since he could not do it right away, the monk left the room with a bow.

In the next few days, he tried to strike the gong with one hand and also attempted to play different musical instruments with one hand in front of the master, but the latter told him none was right.

Finally, it is said that he reached enlightenment by declaring, "I have heard sound without sound."

In this case, the master wanted to convey to the monk that physical phenomenon surrounding us is just the mental interpretation of outside stimuli. Without a recipient outside objects are neither ex-

isting nor non-existing. This case has demonstrated
that our mental faculties can even create their own
images independent of outside stimuli. In our own
mind, such imaginary sound is as real as the actual
vibration of air waves bombarding our eardrums.

Case History 4
You Poured Too Much Tea

There was a man who went to see a master
about Zen. Instead of listening, this man kept talking about his own ideas. After awhile, the master
served tea. He kept on pouring tea into his visitor's
cup even though it was already full.

Finally, the visitor could not restrain himself.
"Don't you see it's full?" he said, "and it can't hold
any more."

"Exactly," replied the master and stopped pouring at last. "Like this cup, you are filled with your
own ideas. How can you expect me to tell you about
Zen unless you offer me an empty cup?"

This episode is comparatively easy to understand. It is impossible to impart anything if you are
preoccupied already. In a situation like this, it is
quite adequate to compare a tea cup with our
receptacle of knowledge.

Case History 5
A Gosling in the Bottle

Most of our problems are created by our own
thoughts. We are trapped by our own system of
thinking, and hence in a dilemma. The following
case is a good illustration.

An official asked a master to explain to him the old problem of a goose in a bottle.

"A man puts a gosling into the bottle," the official said, "and feeds the gosling through the bottleneck until it grows and becomes a goose. Finally, there is no more room inside for the goose to grow. How can the man get the goose out without killing it or breaking the bottle?"

"Sir!" shouted the master and clapped his hands.

"Yes, master!"

"Look!" said the master, "The goose is out."

In vertical thinking, we confine our reasoning process either to breaking the bottle or to squeezing the goose out. In the latter case, we cannot guarantee that the goose will stay alive. There seems to be no other way out other than these two.

In lateral thinking, we also check if the problem is the fabrication of our own thinking, and see if we are trapped by it. Since the problem itself can never exist in reality, it obviously is a creation of our own mind. So the easiest way out is to shout the non-existing goose out of the non-existing bottle and the non-existing problem is satisfactorily solved, and you psychologically feel better.

Have we ever examined in our daily life, how many problems we are confronted with belong to this category, and the frustrations we experience are due to our own imagination?

Case History 6
How to Control Your Temper

There was a student who came to a master for instruction. His problem was how to get rid of his violent temper.

"Show me this temper," said the master. "It sounds very fascinating."

"Since I haven't got it now, I can't show it to you," said the student.

"Well then, bring it to me when you have it."

"But I can't bring it to you when I have it. I'd lose it before I got to show you," answered the student.

"If this is the case," said the master, "it seems to me that this violent temper of yours is not a part of your nature. If it is not a part of you, it must come into you from outside. I suggest that whenever it gets into you, you spank yourself with a stick until the temper can't stand it and runs away."

This case gives us some insight into human nature. If we look inward and introspect ourselves regularly and diligently, violent tempers as well as other manifestations of emotional disturbances such as neurosis and psychosis can be easily uprooted. Thus, in the field of mental health, this little story can serve quite effectively as a form of psycho-therapy.

Case History 7
Where Did Your Anger Come

One Chinese Zen master remarked, "When I began to study Zen, mountains were mountains; when I thought I understood Zen, mountains were not mountains; but when I came to the full

75

knowledge of Zen, mountains were again mountains."

The following story is a good case to illustrate such a view.

There was another young student who went to visit a master. In order to impress the master, he said, "There is no mind; there is no body; there is no Buddha. There is no master, and there is no student. Nothing is good and nothing is bad. What we see and feel is not real. All that is real is emptiness. No physical phenomena really exists."

The master had been sitting quietly listening. Now he picked up his stick and without any warning gave the young man a good spanking. The latter jumped up in anger.

"Since none of these things really exist, and all is emptiness," said the master, "where did your anger come from? Think about it."

We know that on the atomic level, everything is not differentiated; but on the physical level, everything should be treated as it is. For instance, if you are ill, you have to recognize that you are ill. If you see a mountain, you cannot ignore that it is a mountain. What is important is that on the phenomenal level, we should have the concept of "suchness". We should recognize things as they are. There are two kinds of truth: one is the apparent truth, and the other is ultimate truth. We should neither ignore one of them nor should we take one for another. In other words, we should never confuse the levels of abstraction at any time.

Case History 8
There Is Nothing In Zen

One student worked in a monastery doing menial labor for quite a few years. He hoped to get some instruction in Zen. He asked one of his fellow students what to do.

His friend said, "Go inside and ask the master."

So he went in."I have been working here as a laborer for many years and never had a chance to receive any instruction from you in Zen. Could you tell me something about it?" requested the student.

"I am busy now," replied the master.

Consequently, the student left and told his friend about the interview. His friend suggested he should go inside again.

He went inside and made the same request.

"I told you I am busy," the master said quite impatiently. "Don't bother me again."

The student was much disappointed. He left the office and again told his friend what the master had said.

His friend said, "In order to show your sincerity, you must insist on your request. I am sure this time he will give you a lecture on Zen."

So for the third time, he went in and repeated the same request.

The master, instead of giving him a lecture on Zen, picked up his stick and gave him a few whacks and demanded him to go outside. This time, being really angry, the student shouted, "I suspect you have nothing to teach me."

At this point, the master asked the student what he had just said.

"I said you have nothing to teach me," said the student.

"You are enlightened," remarked the master.

This dialogue looks very odd at first. The student showed his earnestness and seriousness, but the master seemed to be very reluctant to instruct him. If, however, we study this unusual dramatic episode carefully, we can grasp the profound truth of Buddhistic philosophy. Since we know that Buddha nature is within each of us, and that language cannot transfer any meaning adequately, therefore, nobody really can teach anybody else about enlightenment. In other words, enlightenment is strictly a matter of self-realization. This dialogue has revealed to us this truth.

Case History 9
Where is Buddha?

"Where is Buddha?" one student asked his master.

"Where does your question come from?" replied the master.

In the Zen dialogue, the use of a question as an answer is sometimes used. It serves the following purposes:

1. To give an answer,
2. To rebuff the question, and
3. To make you ponder over your own question again.

Case History 10
A Beautiful Girl

Two young monks were walking down a muddy street in the city. There came a beautiful girl who was trying to cross the street in her neat dress. One monk offered to help her across the street.

In the evening, the other monk remarked to the first monk, "Monks are not supposed to be near any female body, certainly not that beautiful girl you helped in the city."

The first monk replied, "I have put that girl down way back in the city. It is you who still have the girl in your mind."

This episode is self-explanatory. No interpretation is necessary.

The cases stated above are merely a few examples of lateral thinking. There are thousands of cases mentioned in the Chinese book entitled *Record of Transmission of Light* (傳燈錄) which is an anthology of biographies of Buddhist masters comprising over 1701 entries. These cases are known as public cases (公案 pronounced *kung an* in Chinese or koan in Japanese). Among these public cases, some are very difficult to interpret. They still baffle the thinking faculties of the average man. A separate book exclusively investigating, classifying, and interpreting these cases should be written in the future, so that lateral thinking or non-Aristotelian logic may have its due place in man's quest for ultimate truth.

Chapter 13

Mantra as Physical Therapy

If a person does not speak to other people, sing or hum to himself for a certain length of time, say for one or two days, he may experience a dammed up feeling. Such feeling is not just psychological, such as a feeling of solitude. It is physiological as well. Because not only one's speech apparatus does not have the needed exercise, one's internal organs also lack the effect of vibration which results from vocalization. It would be ideal, if we could devise a way that by vocalizing certain vowels, dipthongs, and consonant-vowel combinations, the sound vibrations could definitely effect different internal organs.

Such a way is in actuality being practiced in Buddhistic devotion. It is called mantra. Mantra is based on certain vowel combinations which are chanted in a specific manner so as to produce a vibrating effect on the brain, glands, nerves and indeed the entire system of those who practice it.

For example:

1. "i" (as in bee) is a front vowel with the tongue position held up. The sustained vocalization of this vowel can vibrate all the organs situated in the skull. It can clear the brain, eyes, nose and ears and can also give an exhilarating feeling.

2. "e" (as in wet) is a front vowel with the tongue position held neither high nor low. The sustained

vocalization of this vowel can affect the area of the throat, larynx, trachea, etc.

3. "a" (as in glass, last) is a low front vowel. Vocalizing this vowel can benefit the upper lung.

4. "ə " (as in flirt) is a mid vowel. It works on the diaphragm, liver and stomach.

The "OM" or "AUM" sound is considered spiritually important. It is claimed to embrace the voice production of the entire range of human speech. By analyzing human speech organs, such a claim is quite justified."A" and "u" are two back vowels, one being the high one, the other the low one. "M" is a libial consonant. No other sounds can be produced further than "m" sound. In other words, all other sounds are produced between these three sounds. Therefore, you can say the "AUM" sound includes all human speech sounds.

If vibration, just like massage, is a form of exercise and is beneficial to our physical well-being, then it is particularly important to our internal organs because otherwise we have no access to them.

Therefore, while we may not agree with the benefit of mantras on the metaphysical level, we should not, however, ignore their benefit on the physical level. It is reported in Devi's book, *Forever Young, Forever Healthy* that voice therapy has been carried out experimentally by a medical doctor in Germany. In this country, voice production as physical therapy has not been recognized yet.

This writer believes theoretically it is possible that by focusing voice production at different vocal points in the speech mechanism we produce effects on different internal organs. Mantra, hence, can be employed as an effective means of physical therapy for certain illnesses. The author also believes that clinical work should be instituted and more scientific investigation should be conducted in this area to see what potentiality voice therapy has in alleviating human suffering, which is Buddha's basic concern.

Chapter 14

Tai Chi Ch'uan

It seems odd at first glance that in a book on philosophy, , a health program is included. We must agree, however, that nobody can be happy unless he is healthy. In order to be healthy, mental health as well as physical health are equally important. The Buddhistic outlook on life can take care of mental health. But physical training and nutrition must be instituted in order to promote physical health.

We are interested in man's well-being in its totality. A feeble body can only produce a feeble mind. With a feeble mind we can never think deep enough to fathom the truth or make any advancement on the spiritual path. To include a chapter of tai chi ch'uan in this book is just like to include hatha yoga, the yoga of physical well-being, in yoga philosophy.

This chapter will inform the reader of how tai chi ch'uan, a health program, was historically related to Buddhism, and what benefit we can derive from it. This chapter will also inform the reader, regretfully, the difficulties confronted by the printed word in illustrating the physical movements of tai ch'i ch'uan, and finally how we can overcome such difficulties.

What is Tai Chi Ch'uan?

Tai chi ch'uan is a health system which includes one set of exercises made up of approximately 96 postures. They are slow, continuous, and rhythmic movements that can promote our health and stretch our life span. It has been developed for many thousands of years, and has been perfected for over 700 years.

To perform the whole set of tai chi ch'uan takes about 15 minutes. Every time after practice, we feel refreshed, as if every cell in our body is charged with new energy. Our mind is collected, and our spirit lifted. We feel a new joy and a serene strength within us. We carry this newly acquired joy and strength to our other daily activities. They increase our work efficiency, improve our mental alertness, and calm our nervous tension.

To do this set of exercises, no equipment is necessary. We can practice alone, even in secret, if we like. A little space will be sufficient. It is good for both men and women, young and old alike. It is particularly suitable for older people who cannot participate in other strenuous sports, since this system teaches us only slow and gentle movements.

Origin and Development of Tai Chi Ch'uan

Modern scientists conduct their scientific investigations and inquiries by observing and analyzing the problem. They use inductive and deductive methods in order to expand man's frontier of knowledge. Ancients in China, as elsewhere, almost did the same thing, except that at that time there was less scientific data at their disposal.

Those ancients were amazed by certain physical phenomena. They wondered, for instance, why in the animal kingdom, certain lower species had so much strength and vitality, even outliving man. They watched these animals' bodily movements, hoping that by imitating their characteristic movements, they too, could acquire such desirable traits. They followed these animals' postures in their exercises just like modern scientists shape their airplanes after birds, and ships after fish.

About 2200 years ago, five types of *ch'uan* or exercises were in existence: namely, dragon ch'uan, tiger ch'uan, leopard ch'uan, snake ch'uan, and crane ch'uan. These were simple exercises featuring these animals' postures in order to strengthen man's physique, and to prolong man's life.

As time went on, these exercises were improved and expanded. They were chiefly practiced by Buddhist monks living at the famous Shao Lin Monastery in China. The reason why Buddhist monks underwent such physical training was because they sat still meditating for hours each day. It was necessary for them to move around and do some physical exercise in order to keep fit. The improved version of these exercises was known as the Shao Lin School in the history of Chinese physical education.

This source of physical training had direct bearing on the development of tai chi ch'uan, which was credited to be the creation of a man named Chang Sanfeng.

Chang Sanfeng, known as the father of tai chi ch'uan, was a Taoist. He was born in 1247 A.D. His exact date of death is unknown. He was well versed in Shao Lin exercise and Taoist breathing technique, which is similar to that of the Buddhists.

Being a Taoist himself, he was particularly aware of the philosophy of yin and yang. That is the Chinese concept of the universe. According to this concept, the universe, just like an atom, is fundamentally composed of two elements, namely, yin and yang, or negative and positive. Anything that is not balanced yin-yang wise, will cause disharmony and eventually disintegrate. To live in accordance with the doctrine of yin-yang is to live in harmony with Tao, the law of nature. This law is intangible and invisible. It is however, the governing force of nature, immutable, eternal, and always in operation.

Chang was a man of imagination and originality. His dramatic creation of tai ch'i ch'uan is just as fascinating as tai ch'i ch'uan itself. One day, according to recorded history, he saw a magpie trying to hit a snake coiled on the ground. The snake, poised but alert, avoided the frontal attack by moving its body a little bit. The bird missed the snake. Frustrated, it flapped its wings, flew into the sky and landed again with a renewed effort. Again, it missed the target. The bird made a few more attempts, but always ended in failure. Finally, as Chang walked close to the battlefield, both the snake and the magpie fled in a hurry.

From this battle scene, Chang deeply realized the subtlety between the two opposite forces at work, the active and the passive, the dominant and the recessive, the force of attack and the power of absorption.

Since he was familiar with the physical training then prevailing, suddenly he conceived a new idea. From that idea he developed a new system of physical culture of his own. This system makes it possible for man to be in tune with nature's vibration while in motion. Its composition is quite complicated; its form highly symbolic; its rhythm very melodic; and above all, its therapeutic value is far superior to any known exercise, ancient or modern, eastern or western.

This unique and most celebrated system has benefited mankind for the last seven hundred years already. In this fast moving world of ours, where the leisurely mode of living is a thing of the past, and relaxation has become a lost art, it seems to be more urgent now than ever before to have this type of exercise serve entire humanity.

Therapeutic Value of Tai Chi Ch'uan

In order to understand and appreciate the therapeutic value and preventive effect of tai chi ch'uan on some health problems, a few words on tai chi breathing are necessary.

Tai chi ch'uan is primarily concerned with man's well being in its totality. Hence its stress differs from other gymnastics such as those planned for muscle building, or those designed for exhibition purposes. The accent of tai chi ch'uan is on the technique of breathing. Proper breathing is an integral part of this system just as music is an integral

87

part of dance. For the advanced students of tai chi every bodily movement has to be coordinated with rhythmic breathing in order to get the maximum effect.

According to tai chi principle, breathing should always be deep, slow, and rhythmic. Inhaling and exhaling must be even. Complete breathing is imperative. That is to say, in the act of inhalation, the air should fill the lower, middle and upper parts of the lung in succession. In the act of exhalation, the air to be emptied starts from the lower part, then the middle part, and finally the upper part.

It is also the basic principle of tai chi breathing that we inhale whenever our hands stretch, rise, or push forward; and that we exhale whenever our hands contract, fall or pull backward.

The most ingenious and unusual part of tai chi ch'uan is that it is constructed in such a way that stretching and contracting, rising and falling, pushing forward and pulling backward of our hands, and to a certain extent, of our body, are always in alteration, and are always in circular and unbroken movements. So that once we are used to this principle, it is quite natural for us to gear our movements to this breathing technique.

The interest of tai chi ch'uan is also centered on the subject of "*ch'i*", which literally means air. *Ch'i* is in the air, but it is not the air nor one of its chemical components. We may consider it as the life giving principle or vital cosmic force. In ordinary breathing, we absorb some amount of *ch'i*, but by controlled or regulated breathing, we absorb more and we store it in the solar plexus. The surplus of ch'i inside, according to the theory of tai chi ch'uan, can be translated into strength and vitality, manifesting itself in perfect health, youthful complexion, and magnetic personality.

It is, of course, not too easy to convince the western public of the existence of "*ch'i*" as such. We should note, however, that even without introducing this new word *ch'i*, the benefits to be derived from the combination of rhythmic breathing and various postures are quite obvious.

In other words, the aim of tai chi breathing is to effectively get the maximum amount of oxygen to all parts of the body. It is just like a program of daily walking or running, lately known as aerobics, except that tai chi ch'uan is a set of more sophisticated exercises. Therefore, it can generate more benefits than walking or running. The basic therapeutic value of tai chi ch'uan is as follows:

1. It is good for the lungs. The lungs may lower their vitality, if they are only partially used all the time. The impairment of vitality renders the system open to attack from disease and germs.

2. It is good for the blood. The blood is refreshed and vitalized because of the large intake of oxygen through complete breathing. The properly oxygenated bloodstream, in turn, promotes health and efficiency of the glandular and nervous systems.

3. It is good for the organs of digestion and elimination. Through deep breathing the diaphragm exerts gentle pressure upon the stomach and other organs in that region. This in-

ternal massage stimulates those organs to function properly.

4. It is good for waist reducing. Since all movements of tai chi ch'uan originate from the waist, this region naturally gets plenty of exercise. Therefore, extra pounds in the body, particularly in this area, can be cut to a minimum.

5. It is good for the entire physical body. Tai chi ch'uan is a set of balanced exercises. While practicing, the body is in a completely relaxed state. Every vital organ in the body can, therefore, greatly benefit from the combined effect of rhythmic breathing and various postures.

6. It is good for the mind. The execution of tai chi ch'uan requires deep concentration. It makes the mind calm and serene. Nervous people and those who do not know the art of relaxation will get much out of it after a short period of practice.

Caution should be given here that breathing coordinated with postures is for advanced students only. Beginners are discouraged to put their attention on breathing for the very reason that their unfamiliarity with and hence constant delay of the external postures may interfere with normal rhythmic breathing. In the first stage of learning, breathing should be automatic, spontaneous and unconscious. Unless and until students have mastered the external form, they should not be ushered into the internal discipline.

Students at the beginning stage will get their due reward as they progress on the path, since every time the entire body is exercised during the execution of tai chi ch'uan, the mind is brought into play. The pleasant effort they spend will have a lasting effect in relaxing their body and mind. Furthermore, the interim period will also strengthen weaker people to a certain degree, so that they may have a safer way for more advanced work.

The New Pedagogical Problem and Its Solution

Since tai chi ch'uan is a performing art, it is humanly impossible to show how it is done in printed words. Even the drawings cannot tell the whole story adequately because by looking at separate drawings, the reader still cannot figure out how the transition takes place from one posture to another. In China, many people practice this art. It is, therefore, quite easy to find a teacher there. On the other hand, the shortage of tai chi ch'uan instructors outside China does pose a serious problem for those who are interested in this program of physical fitness.

Fortunately, there are now audio-visual equipment available as teaching devices. Among these facilities, film and television can be employed as the most effective devices for teaching tai chi ch'uan in the absence of an instructor. Recently, in the United States, tai chi ch'uan studios have been available in the big cities such as New York, San Francisco, Los Angeles, and Honolulu. Interested parties should consult local telephone directories for more information.

Finally, there are three points which the reader should bear in mind.

1. In former days, on account of the lack of standard teaching devices such as motion pictures, there emerged a few schools teaching different styles of tai chi ch'uan. But their teachings are based on the same principles and hence, the benefits to be derived are virtually identical.

2. Although tai chi ch'uan had its origin in Taoism, yet those who practice it now have different religious affiliations. Generally, people practice it just for the sake of health. If the practitioner happens to be a Buddhist, that is purely coincidental.

3. Tai chi ch'uan is a form of art. The performer can always find aesthetic satisfaction each time his routine is executed, and thus will never result in boredom or monotony.

Chapter 15

Buddhistic Dietary Rules vs. Modern Nutritional Science

Before Buddha was enlightened, he practiced austere self-discipline for salvation. He tortured himself patiently by suppressing the wants of life for six years. However, his fasts did not advance him in his search for salvation. On the other hand, his body was so weak that he almost died from malnutrition. When he saw that it was not the right way, he abandoned it and instead adopted the middle path.

After his enlightenment, he advised people not to seek salvation in austerities nor to indulge in worldly pleasures. As far as food intake goes, he advised people to eat and drink what they need.

In the light of this advice, let us examine these questions: Is our food intake adequate in nutrition? Is our food balanced?

We are supposed to live in an affluent society. Why then are there so many people plagued by high blood pressure, heart trouble, alcoholic and weight problems? Since we are what we eat, there must be something wrong with our diet.

In this country, people buy what they eat in grocery stores or supermarkets where most food items have been over-refined and over-processed. Many food items are sold in cans. It is true that canned food can keep for a long time. It has commercial value. But its food value is impoverished. The greens sold in the markets are no longer from organic soil. In short, the food we consume is no longer the food people used to have when they had their own self-sustaining farms.

Furthermore, our diet is not balanced. We consume too much starch, such as, potato, bread and cakes. We consume too much sugar, for instance, sugar in coffee, sugar in dessert, sugar in baked goods, sugar in soft drinks, in short, sugar everywhere. In addition to the hidden sugar consumed, we again eat candy for all occasions.

On top of these, there is another problem confronting the modern man. We eat a lot of starch and sugar while we lead a sedentary life. We push buttons instead of doing menial labor. We watch football games and other sports instead of actively participating in them. We use automobiles to drive around instead of walking. The fact is if we do not have enough physical exercise, the starch and sugar we have cannot transform into energy but stays in the body as fat.

Since health is of paramount importance to everyone of us, and Buddha has emphasized that we should eat and drink whatever our body needs, let us then implement his view on food and nutrition taking into account the special environment we live in.

According to recent findings in nutritional research, we need 40 nutrients which cannot be made in the body; namely:

<u>10 proteins</u>: Our body is largely made up of proteins, which are made up of amino acids.

<u>14 minerals</u>: Minerals can serve as building material for bones and teeth or act as body regulators.

<u>15 vitamins</u>: Vitamins are chemicals which are essential for the normal functioning of cells.

<u>1 essential fatty acid.</u>

From these 40 nutrients our bodies synthesize an estimated 10,000 different compounds essential to the maintenance of health. Among these compounds some 3,000 are already known. Deficiency in any nutrient, therefore, may result in the underproduction of hundreds of these essential compounds.

According to authorities in this field, we need five groups of food:

1. <u>Grain products</u>: inexpensive sources of energy and proteins. Whole grains carry iron and certain vitamins.

2. <u>Fats and sugar</u>: good sources of energy. Some fats also carry vitamins.

3. <u>Meats, poultry, fish, eggs, legumes and nuts</u>: valuable sources of protein, some minerals and vitamins.

4. <u>Milk and dairy products</u>: valuable sources of protein, calcium, other minerals and vitamins.

5. <u>Vegetables and fruits</u>: chiefly important as sources of vitamins and minerals.

From what is mentioned above, we can see that animal flesh is rich in protein. However, too much animal fat may coagulate in our arteries and cause high blood pressure and heart trouble. On the other hand, Buddhists are vegetarians. They deplore meat eating or use of any animal fat in cooking. They impose such strict dietary rules on themselves because they deeply believe in the reverence for life. Since they themselves do not want to suffer, they feel it is not right to inflict suffering upon other poor animals by slaughtering them.

Aside from this humanitarian view, if a person abstains from meat eating, does he get enough proteins? Yes, if he uses meat substitutes. People in this country know that meat is rich in proteins, but most are not aware of the fact that the protein in soybeans is just as rich as that in any kind of meat.

In China, where soybeans are abundant and their prices low, most people are dependent on these beans and their endless by-products for their proteins. In this country, soybeans are not a staple food. Soy oil is not saturated like animal fat. It contains Vitamin E which is good for the heart. Soybeans also contain lecithin which is an essential acid that can break up fatty deposits in the arteries and thus facilitate the cure of high blood pressure and cholesterol problems. In China, people drink soy milk instead of cow's milk because its price is only a fraction of cow's milk, its smell is delicious, and above all, it is not as mucous forming as cow's milk.

The comparative value in nutrition between 85 grams of oven cooked roast beef and soybeans can be seen from the analysis in Diagram 4.

Note that there is no saturated fatty acid in soy beans whatsoever. According to the latest findings

beef	soybeans	nutrient
85g	85g	
390	355	calories
16g	30g	protein
-	26g	carbohydrate
-	2.2g	fiber
36g	17g	fat
35g	-	saturated fatty acid
-	85g	linoleic acid
2.1mg	6.8mg	iron
7mg	168 mg	calcium
105mg	474mg	phosphorus
350mg	1,411mg	potassium
60mg	0.8 mg	sodium
60 units	93.5 units	Vitamin A
-	0.7 mg	Vitamin B_1
-	0.2 mg	Vitamin B_2
3mg	1.8 mg	niacin

Diagram 4. COMPARISON OF THE NUTRI-
TIONAL VALUES BETWEEN BEEF AND
SOYBEANS

in nutrition, all atherosclerosis is characterized by an increase of blood cholesterol and decrease in lecithin. Lecithin can keep the blood fat at normal levels, and soybeans are a rich source of lecithin.

No wonder monks who are strict vegetarians do not have cholesterol problems. Even the general public in the Orient who acquires their protein from some meat and a lot of soy bean products and who consume soy oil and other vegetable oils instead of animal fat and hydrogenated fat are free from high blood pressure or heart trouble. Since they cannot afford the luxury of private automobiles and have to walk most of the time to get anywhere, they do not have weight problems either.

Just eating a lot of nutrients without discretion will not make us healthy. Because some nutrients, particularly the vitamin B group are synergistic, namely, if one kind of nutrient is taken in excess, the body needs another kind to balance before it can assimilate properly. In natural foods this problem is automatically taken care of. Therefore, in a culture, where natural food is available, just follow nature. The natural way is always the best way.

But in a place where natural food is not generally available, namely, where most of food items are over-processed and over-polished, then we have to use our discriminating faculties for our food intake. In order to be healthy, the science of nutrition becomes everyone's business.

Hence, as far as nutrition is concerned, the way to health is twofold:

1. We must acquire all nutrients our body needs;

2. We must have the correct proportion for each nutrient.

Finally, we can arrive at the following conclusion. From the view of Buddhistic dietary rules, we should deplore the slaughter of animals and abstain from meat eating. From the point of modern nutritional science, a well-planned vegetarian diet can meet the needs of our body adequately.

AFTERWORD

In this phenomenal world, everything is changing; nothing is permanent. In our society, the pace of living is so fast, and we are so busy. We hardly have time to think. If we can take a few minutes out from our busy schedule everyday and dwell on the notion of truth, peace or eternity, what a blessing that would be!

It would be even better if we could take a few minutes out everyday to just relax, without letting anything bother us, without thinking about anything, not even the notion mentioned above. In this way, we are already on the right path of meditation which is the objective of this book.

----------END----------

BIBLIOGRAPHY

I. BOOKS IN ENGLISH

BUDDHISM

1. Burtt, E.A., ed., *The Teachings of the Compassionate Buddha*, New York: The New American Library, 1955.
2. Carus, Paul, *The Gospel of Buddha: Compiled from Ancient Records*, Chicago: The Open Court Publishing Company, 1915.
3. Ch'en, Kenneth K.S., *Buddhism: the Light of Asia*, New York: Barron's Educational Series, Inc., 1968.
4. Conze, Edward, *Buddhist Texts Through the Ages*, New York: Philosophical Library, 1954.
5. Coomaraswamy, Ananda K., *Hinduism and Buddhism*, New York: Philosophical Library.
6. LuZanne, Celina, *Heritage of Buddha: The Story of Siddhartha Gautama*, New York: Philosophical Library, 1953.
7. Miura, Isshu and Sasaki, Ruth Fuller, *The Zen Koan: Its History and Use in Rinzai Zen*, New York: Harcourt, Brace and World, Inc., 1965.
8. *Sayings of Buddha*, New York: The Peter Pauper Press, 1957.
9. Suzuki, Daisetz Teitaro, *Studies in Zen*, New York: Philosophical Library, 1955.
10. *Zen Buddhism*, New York: The Peter Pauper Press, 1959.

GENERAL SEMANTICS

11. Chase, Stuart, *Power of Words*, New York: Harcourt, 1954.
12. Chase, Stuart, *The Tyranny of Words*, New York: Harcourt, 1938.
13. Hayakawa, Samuel, *General Semantics*, New York: Harcourt, 1963.
14. Hayakawa, Samuel, *Language in Thought and Action*, New York: Harcourt, 1964.
15. Korzybski, Alfred, *Manhood of Humanity*: *The Science and Art of Human Engineering*, New York: E. P. Dutton & Co., 1921.
16. Korzybski, Alfred, *Science and Sanity*:*An Introduction to Non-Aristotelian Systems and General Semantics*.
17. Lee, Irving J., *Language Habits in Human Affairs*: *an Introduction to General Semantics, with a forward by Alfred Korzybski*, New York: Harper & Brothers, 1941.

SCIENCE
18. Halacy, D., *Popular Electronics*,"Biological Radio, ESP", Apr. 1967.
19. Needham, Joseph, *Science and Civilization in China*, New York: Cambridge University, 1954.
20. White, Harvey E., *Classical and Modern Physics*, New York: D. Van Nostrand Company, Inc., 1940.

YOGA
21. Arunachalam, Ponnambalam, Sir, *Light from the East*: *Being Letters on Gnana, the Divine Knowledge*, London: Allen & Unwin, 1927.

22. Bhikshu, *A Series of Lessons in Bhakti Yoga, the Only Book on the Rationale of Bkakti Yoga*, Chicago: Yogi Publication Society, 1930.

23. Brunton, Paul, *The Hidden Teaching Beyond Yoga*, New York: E. P. Dutton & Co., Inc., 1942.

24. Grewal, Singh, *Risha Patanjali's Raja Yoga: A Revelation of the Science of Yoga with Commentary*, 1935.

25. *Light on the Path*, Pasadena, CA: Theosophical University Press, 1949.

26. Paramananda, Swami, *Concentration and Meditation*, Boston: The Vedanta Center, 1933.

27. Prabhavananda, Swami and Isherwood Christopher, trans., *Bhagavad Gita*, New York: The New American Library, 1951.

28. Sri Deva Ram Sukul, *Yoga and Self-culture: A Scientific and Practical Survey of a Yoga Philosophy for the Layman and the Aspirant on the Path*, New York: Yoga Institute of America, 1947.

29. Vivekananda, Swami, *Karma-yoga and Bhakti-yoga*, New York: Ramakrishna-Vevekananda Center, 1955.

30. Vivekananda, Swami, *Raja-yoga or Conquering the Internal Nature*, Almora: Advaita Ashrama, 1928.

31. Wood, Ernest, *Great Systems of Yoga*, New York: Philosophical Society, 1954.

32. Yesudian, Selvarajan, and Haich, Elisabeth, (trans. by John P. Robertson), *Yoga and Health*, New York: Harper and Brothers Publisher, 1953.

33. Ramacharaka, *Hatha Yoga or the Yogi Philosphy of Well-Being*, Chicago: Yogi Publication Society, 1932.

34. Yogi, Ramacharaka, *Science of Breath: A Complete Manual of the Oriental Breathing Philosophy of Physical, Mental, Psychic and Spiritual Development*, Chicago: Yogi Publication Society, 1932.

35. Ramacharaka, *The Science of Psychic Healing*, Chicago: Yogi Publication Society, 1934.

36. Yogi, Ramacharaka, *A Series of Lessons in Gnani Yoga (The Yoga of Wisdom)*, Chicago: The Yogi Publication Society, 1907.

37. Yogananda, Paramhansa, *Autobiography of a Yogi*, Los Angeles: Self-Realization Fellowship, 1946.

GENERAL

38. Corry, J. A., *Elements of Democratic Government*, New York; Oxford University Press, 1947.

39. Davis, Adelle, *Let's Eat Right to Keep Fit*, New York: Harcourt, Brace and Company, 1954.

40. Devi, Indra, *Forever Young Forever Healthy*, New York: Prentice-Hall, Inc. 1953.

41. Gettell, Raymond G., *History of Political Thought*, New York: D. Appleton-Century Company, 1924.

42. Jaspers, Karl, *The Great Philosophers*, New York: Harcourt, 1962.

43. Key, V.O. Jr., *Politics, Parties and Pressure Groups*, New York: Thomas Y. Crowell Company, 1947.

44. Manser, Ruth B. and Finlan, Leonard, *The Speaking Voice*, New York: Longmans, Green and Co., 1950.
45. Noss, John B., *Man's Religion*, New York: The MacMillan Company, 1949.
46. Thorpe, Louis P., *The Psychology of Mental Health*, New York: The Ronald Press Company, 1950.
47. Wallin, J. E. Wallace, *Personality Maladjustment and Mental Hygiene*, New York: McGraw-Hill Book Company, Inc., 1949.
48. Wordsworth, William, *The Prelude: Selected Poems and Sonnets*, New York: Rhinehart and Co., Inc., 1948.
49. Yogananda, Paramhansa, *The Science of Religion*, Los Angeles: Self-realization Publishing House, 1953.

II. BOOKS IN CHINESE
(All titles are romanized in Wade-Giles)

<u>BUDDHISM</u>

1. *Chin Gang Ching,* English title translated as *Diamond Sutra.*

   〔 金剛經〕

2. *Ching Te Ch'uan Deng Lu,* from *P'u Hui Da Tsang Ching* edition, Taipei: Chen Shan Mei Ch'u Pan She, 1967.

   〔<u>景德傳燈錄</u>，<u>普慧大藏經</u>，真善美出版社〕

3. Chu Yun Fa Shih, *Fo Chiao Yu Chi Tu Chiao Te Pi Chiao,* Hong Kong: Hua Ch'eng Shu Chu.

   〔 煮雲法師，<u>佛教與基督教的比較</u>，華成書局〕

4. Huang Shih Fu, *Fo Chiao Kai Lun,* Hong Kong: Shang Wu Yin Shu Kuan.

   〔 黃士復，<u>佛教概論</u>，　商務印書館〕

5. Li Ching T'ong, *Yin Guang Da Shih Wen Ch'ao Jing Hua Lu,* Hong Kong: Fo Ching Yin Song Ch'u.

   〔 李淨通，<u>印光大師文鈔菁華錄</u>，佛經印送處〕

6. *Liu Tsu Fa Bao T'an Ching* or *The Sutra Spoken by the Sixth Patriarch,* told by Master Fa Hai, Hong Kong: Fuo Ching Liu Tong Ch'u.

   〔 法海大師，<u>六祖法寶壇經</u>，佛經流通處〕

7. Long Shu P'u Sa, *Da Chih Tu Lun*, Taipei: Chen Shan Mei Ch'u Pan She, 1967.

（龍樹菩薩，大智度論上，下，真善美出版社）

8. *Mi Chiao T'ong Kuan*, Taipei: Tzu You Ch'u Pan She, 1965.

（密教通關，臺北：自由出版社）

9. You Chih Piao, *Fo Chiao Ke Hsieuh Kuan*, Hong Kong: Fo Ching Yin Song Chu.

（尤智表，佛教科學觀，佛經印送處）

CLASSICAL PHILOSOPHY

10. *Chong Yong*　（中庸）
11. *Chuang Tzu*　（莊子）
12. *Da Hsiueh*　（大學）
13. Kong Tzu, *Lun Yu*　（孔子，論語）
14. Lao Tzu, *Tao Te Ching*　（老子，道德經）
15 *Meng Tzu*　（孟子）
16. *Yi Ching*　（易經）

TAI CHI CH'UAN

17. Long Tzu Hsiang, *Tai Chi Ch'uan Hsueh*, Kowloon: Ma Chin Chi Shu Chu.

（龍子祥，太極拳學，馬錦記書局）

18. *Tai Chi Ch'uan Tu Shuo*, Hong Kong: Tai Ping Shu Chu, 1962.

（太極拳圖説，太平書局）

19. Chen Wei Ming, *Tai Chi Da Wen*, Shanghai: Chih Rou Ch'uan She, 1927.

（陳微明，太極答問，致柔拳社）

20. Wu Tu Nan, *Tai Ch'i Ch'uan,* Changsha: Shan Wu Yin Shu Kuan, 1938.

（吳圖南，太極拳，商務印書館）

21. *Wu Chia Tai Ch'i Ch'uan.*

（吳家太極拳）

22. Yang Chen Fu, *Tai Ch'i Ch'uan.*

（楊澄甫，太極拳）

GENERAL.

23. *Chang Sanfeng Ta Tao Chih Yao,* Vol. 5 *Tao Tsang Ching Hua, T*aipei: Tzu You Ch'u Pan She, 1950.

（張三丰，大道指要，道藏精華，自由出版社）

24. Chiang Wei Ch'iao, *Yin Shir Tzu Ching Tsuo Fa.*

（蔣維喬，因是子靜坐法）

25. Feng You Lan, *Chong Kuo Che Hsiueh Shih*..

（馮友蘭，中國哲學史）

26. *Hsin Ching Chian Yao*, Honolulu: Hawaii Chinese Buddhist Society.

（心經講要）

27. *Hsien Hsueh Chen Ch'uan,* Vol. 4, *Tao Tsang Ching Hua,* Taipei: Tzu You Chu' Pan She, 1950.

（<u>仙學真詮</u>，<u>道藏精華</u>，自由出版社）

Index